The Middle Mom

The Middle Mom

HOW TO GROW YOUR HEART BY GIVING IT AWAY

...a foster mom's journey

BY CHRISTIE ERWIN

GRAYSON
PUBLICATIONS
LITTLE ROCK, ARKANSAS

Published by Grayson Publications, P.O. Box 2126, Little Rock, Arkansas 72203. First printing 2009

ISBN 978-0-615-27996-1

Library of Congress Control Number 2009902555

COVER AND LAYOUT DESIGNER:
Kandace Gerber, *Save the Date Designs*

EDITORS: Brenda Buchanan, Fran Taylor, Carolyn Dodds

COVER PHOTOGRAPHER: Maury Draper, *Draper Photography*

INTERIOR PHOTOGRAPHER: Joey Moseley, *Images Photo Design*

WEB DESIGNERS: Chris Steven and Joey Moseley

"Father" SONG WRITER: Carson Harper

For more information about The Middle Mom or to purchase additional copies please visit our website: **www.themiddlemom.com**

This book is dedicated to my precious husband
and children. I love you!

TABLE OF CONTENTS

ACKNOWLEDGMENTS

First and foremost I want to thank the heavenly Father for the incredible honor and opportunity He has given me of being His hands and heart to children in need.

Second, to my parents, Jerry and Sally Johnson, my in-laws, Jerry and Barbara Erwin; and all of the Johnson/Erwin clan, thank you for your unconditional love and support and the countless ways you have undergirded our family on this journey.

I am grateful for all of our friends who have loved on and prayed for the children that God has brought into our home and for the beautiful way they have internalized our ministry as their own.

For my "sisters," Caryl, Donna, and Jan, who have provided shelter for me in the storms of foster care, I love you.

I am indebted to the group of people God has brought together specifically for this project: Kandace Gerber, Maury Draper, Joey Moseley, Carson Harper, Chris Steven, Jennifer and Kevin Wilcox, Fran Taylor, and my Aunt Kaye (for her many hours of editing). You are amazing.

Thank you, Jason Weber, at Hope for Orphans, for your encouragement, enthusiasm and guidance. Most of all, thank you for your commitment to the orphan and for the way you and Trisha practice what you preach. I am blessed to be sharing this journey with you.

I am so thankful for the dedicated people who spend their lives working in the family service field. Thank you for your willingness to navigate the complicated "system" in order to protect and provide for vulnerable children.

To my wonderful husband, Jeff, and my children, Chase,

Caleb, Cara, Connor, and Caroline Serenity, you are my inspiration and a tireless source of compassion and unconditional love. Thank you for embracing God's call on my life and making it your own.

There is no way to adequately thank all of the people involved in both the writing and the living out of this book, but to everyone who has walked with me and encouraged me through this process, I am deeply grateful.

INTRODUCTION

*F*oster care. Those two little words evoke so much emotion in the hearts and minds of Americans. It seems as if only the horror stories of abuse and neglect make the news, and that many of the foster parents in the media are portrayed as greedy deadbeats who use foster children for a "free-ride." Even the hardest of hearts will break at a headline that reads "Foster child molested by foster parent" or "Foster child abused by the very people that were supposed to keep him safe." It's painful. It's unexplainable. It just should not be. But, unfortunately, the small minority that make the ten o'clock news put a negative spin on this important issue. For every so-called "bad" foster parent, there are hundreds, even thousands, of foster parents who are called to this ministry and see it as their life's work; who give their all to serve, protect, nurture, pray for, and love the children that are theirs only for a time.

Foster care is not for everyone. But, it is every believer's job to care for the fatherless, to care for the orphan. In fact, James 1:27 says, "This is pure and undefiled religion in the sight of our God and Father, to visit orphans and widows in their distress, and to keep oneself unstained by the world." If "visiting widows and orphans in their distress" is pure and undefiled religion in God's sight, shouldn't that be good enough for me?

Foster care plays a critical and necessary role in our society, both in adoption and in crisis intervention. In adoption, waiting periods and legal issues sometimes cause a child to be placed in foster care. In crisis intervention, there are times when a child is just not safe in his/her home, whether because of drugs, alcohol, abuse or neglect; and the state Department of Human Services must intervene. The aim of foster care is to be a temporary safe haven for a child who is experiencing the ramifications of his/her parents' actions. Foster care bridges the gap, so to speak, between parent and child while the system attempts to rehabilitate the family. I can't tell you how many times I have heard criticism about how our government handles the foster care system; and in all honesty, I've been the critic at times. But, if we get down to the truth, the real nitty-gritty truth, it is not the government's job to care for the fatherless. It just isn't. The government isn't commissioned, the government isn't commanded, the government isn't equipped, and the government isn't empowered by the One who made it all to care for His children. The church is. We are the people that God has instructed to be different and to make a difference.

According to the United States Department of Health and Human Services; The AFCARS Report; Administration for Children and Families for Fiscal Year 2006, at the end of September 2006, there were 510,000 children in foster care in the United States. Of those, 129,000 were available for adoption. Each one of these children an individual, a divine creation filled with limitless potential, waiting for someone to reach out. Each one of these children has entered foster care through no fault of his/her own and deserve the opportunity to be all that God has created him/her to be.

It is my desire for you to see a different side of foster care: the real meat of what is involved, the heart of foster care. It is my desire for you to see my heart as I attempt to make myself vulnerable and transparent as I share my story. It is one of calling, surrender, doubt, and urgency; of extreme joy and palpable sorrow. It is also just the story of a mother, not a birth mother or a forever mother, but one who fills the gap in a child's life for whatever reason and for whatever length of time and determines to give her heart away in the process: the middle mom. This is by no means a guide to foster parenting, nor do I pretend to be an expert or have all of the answers. My hope is that sharing this ministry will exalt the heavenly Father and perhaps encourage you to reach out to the fatherless in your city or state who are in desperate need of feeling God's loving touch, His tender embrace, and His unconditional love and mercy through you.

The Call

*F*or as long as I can remember, I've loved babies — just loved them. You know the type: a baby can't be within a 3-foot radius without us "baby-lovers" pointing and oohing and cooing in the baby's direction as we wait to be asked if we want to "hold him/her". We're the ones who shop for baby clothes and buy baby-name books, even when we don't have a baby. We volunteer to work in the church nursery, if we can work with the "bed babies" that is. We don't mind changing diapers or getting spit up on. We babysit on Saturday night. Babies R Us. We just love babies. If you are one of us, you know what I mean!

What I didn't realize in all my years of loving babies is that God gave me that love for a purpose and He was going to use that love in a miraculous way in my life. And just for the sake of full disclosure, I have to be honest and say that I have always loved African American babies the best! It could be the residue of my childhood dream to be a black singer, a dream that was shattered when my mom (who believed I could do anything God wanted me to do) gently told me that this dream could never be realized because...well, I was white. That said, God has even used and continues to use that specific love to lead me, change me, and transform me into who He wants me to be.

It is also no coincidence that I was born into my family. My parents were and are the ultimate example of nurture and unconditional love. They are the most loving, genuine people I know and they always seem to know what I need even before I do. They listen: to each other, to their children, their grandchildren and most importantly to the Father. For as long as they have lived, He has guided them through their daily lives, through their years in church ministry, and through some tough personal situations. There is nothing they wouldn't do for me, and I know it. They are my greatest champions. And I am theirs. Their example is the foundation that my entire life and ministry are built upon. For that I am exceedingly grateful.

My foster care journey began on a January day in 1993. It was a day that would define the rest of my life. My husband, Jeff, and I had three children at the time: our son Chase was five, our son Caleb was two and a half, and our daughter Cara was a year old. Unbelievably, the house was quiet that afternoon as the boys slept and I rocked Cara in the living room. As I sat there, cherishing the precious time with my precious girl, my mind began to wander. I thought about how blessed I was to be sitting there in the warmth of our home holding this unbelievable gift. I thought about all of the women who were dying to have a child in their arms. I thought about all of the women who had chosen to end their pregnancies in abortion because they had nowhere else to turn or no one to turn to. Then I thought about all of the children who weren't in anyone's arms that afternoon or any other afternoon, children who lived life without the love of a mother or father, who weren't valued and without God's intervention, they would never be valued in this life. Tears came. My heart broke. And then it was as if God began to speak clearly to me — I mean in an audible voice, in a way I had never experienced. What He said was crystal clear, "It's time for you, my child, to do more than say you are pro-life. It is time to put some action behind those sometimes empty pro-life words." Wow! A song began to come together and flow out of my mouth. It was a song that would change my destiny:

He will never see the sunrise, or hear a robin sing,
He will never drive a sports car, or give a girl a ring.
He will never fish with Daddy, or hold onto Mommy's hand,
'Cause you see this little baby boy will never get the chance.

Please don't take the children;
Don't take the children.
It's up to you to keep them alive.
Please don't take the children;
Don't take the children.
If you do, they will not survive.

She will never see the ocean, or feel a puppy's fur
She will never have a family, 'cause no one's heard of her.
She will never snuggle in your arms on a cold and rainy night,
Or beg you in that tender voice to please, leave on the light.
She will never get to tell you how proud she is of you,
For you see, this little baby girl will never be born to you.

Please don't take the children;

Don't take the children.
It's up to you to keep them alive.
Please don't take the children;
Don't take the children.
If you do, they will not survive.

You say more every day,
That no one understands,
And that this little child inside of you
Just isn't what you'd planned.
You're filled with desperation,
And you don't know what to do.
But, God knows that little baby, and
He'll take care of you.

Please don't take the children;
Don't take the children.
It's up to you to keep them alive.
Please don't take the children;
Don't take the children.
If you do, they will not survive.
If you choose, they cannot survive.

So, there it was. I wrote it down, and when Jeff came home from work, I sang it to him. Now, this was not a typical afternoon welcome, "Come on in honey, let me sing you a song!" His response was, "Where did you hear that?" And with that, I began to tell him about my experience that afternoon. I told him in great detail about what I had heard my heavenly Father say, the deep passion and emotion that had welled up within me, and the undeniable sense that I was being called to action, called out for a mission greater than myself. What action? I had no idea.

Over the next few months, Jeff and I begin to pray, and pray, and pray about where this new "road" would lead us. It was always on my mind, ever present in my thoughts, prayers, and dreams. I knew beyond a shadow of a doubt that God was at work in my heart and life, taking me to a place I had never been before. This was an extremely personal time of searching, of seeking, and of introspection.

Finally, we were led to a private non-profit Christian adoption agency that provided services for young women with unplanned pregnancies; services that included counseling, shepherding homes (where the young woman could live until she delivered her baby), interim care for newborns waiting to be placed with their forever families, and adoption services for families wanting to adopt. This sounded like a perfect fit. I called and requested a packet about our becoming a shepherding home, thinking that this was what we needed to do — welcome a young woman into our home during a difficult time in her life — to love on her, nurture her, guide her, mentor her. Oh, and while I was at it, I requested the foster care packet, too.

I could not wait to get my hands on those packets! When they arrived in the mail, I devoured them. I read them from cover to cover, and was I surprised how God led me! When I read the criteria and rules for a shepherding home, I realized that it was not the right fit for me. It had nothing to do with mentoring young women in trouble. It had to do with me, with my personality and my inability to be firm or confrontational with a stranger in order to set the appropriate boundaries that would be necessary for the success of this part of the ministry. And then, the foster care packet. Foster care in this sense is not what one traditionally thinks of as foster care. The term should have been defined as "interim care" or "cradle care." In this situation, these parents have not had their children removed from their care; they have chosen to place them for adoption. The mission: our family (if we chose to accept) would care for a newborn baby until that baby was placed in the arms of his/her forever family. The majority of these placements would be for a ten day period, which is the legal waiting period for the birth mother in our state. There might be times when it would be longer if there were certain legal issues, health problems with the baby, or if there was not a family waiting for that child.

Okay, maybe this was it. We finally had a concrete ministry to think about, to discuss, and mainly to pray about. After all the months of searching, we realized that foster care was the answer we had been searching for, the answer to the call that had been indelibly placed on my heart on that winter day.

Baby Christopher,
The Journey Begins

*O*nce we completed all the paper work, answered all of the probing and intrusive questions, had our home study done (to insure we had a flushing toilet and a fire extinguisher), had criminal background checks, took classes and had purchased baby "stuff," the wait began! The good news was that we were approved; the bad news was that the wait began.

Every time the phone rang, I hoped it was the agency calling to tell me there was a baby for us to care for. Finally, one October day, that call came. I cannot tell you how excited I was — I felt like I'd just given birth! I called everyone I could think of. It was a boy and, of course, he was beautiful. When the precious bundle arrived, our lives changed forever.

Our family had the privilege of naming him, just for the time we would have him. Chase, who was in the first grade, named him Christopher, after his best friend at school and Christopher Columbus. And so, there we were settling in to this new ministry with this new little life. I loved every minute of it. I could not wait to get up in the morning to greet my precious little fellow and spend the day caring for him along with the rest of my flock. I basked in the smell of Baby Magic and spent every free moment rocking our little Christopher. I smiled as I thought about how awesome it would be for his forever family to hear about his birth, and I cried as I tried to process the incredible pain of a teenage mother who just wanted a better life for her little son she loved so much. I looked forward to the evenings after I had put my children to bed, when I would just rock and cuddle and hold and pray for this life that God had entrusted to me, even if for only a short time. I poured myself into this new life, and in return, I experienced new life as well: life lived in the center of God's call.

During our first foster care experience, I learned many things. One truth caught me unexpectedly as Jeff and I had Christopher with us in a shoe store one night. A lady saw him and asked me how old he was. I explained that he was only a few days old. I realized she was wondering why I was out shopping for shoes after having just delivered a baby. So, although it is not always my custom, I told her what we were doing and why we were doing it. I am not usually one who is extreme in vocalizing my social or political views, but it was at that moment, standing in a shoe store talking to a total stranger, that I realized what a responsibility God had given to me. That newborn baby in my arms "spoke" louder than any verbal or written word about how God feels about the sanctity of life and how He expects His children to feel!

The time with Christopher was a wonderful sweet time. But eventually the same phone that had brought such jubilation ten days earlier rang again. This time it brought a sinking feeling, a deep hole as I tried with everything that was in me to think about my life, the one without our Christopher. I knew from the beginning that this gift from God belonged to someone else, to the perfect family that God had chosen specifically for him; but somehow, all of the truth in that knowledge failed me as I listened to the caseworker map out the plan, the time, the place, and the ceremony.

His adoptive parents were notified, and we took our little "son" to meet them. We entered the agency, were shown into a room and the door was shut. We were to wait there until we got the signal. I sat nervously holding Christopher, anticipating and yet not knowing what to anticipate. I had bonded with this child as if he had been born to me, and yet tomorrow he'd be gone.

Then I heard weeping. Not from the baby, but from a man in another room behind another closed door, a man who would be the forever father to my tiny "son." Tears came to me too. I looked at Jeff and said, "I don't know if I can do this." What I really wanted to do was scream, "What in the world are WE doing? What have I gotten us in to?" The weeping in the other room grew louder and my heart beat grew stronger. Finally, it was time. The adoption worker gently patted my shoulder and took Christopher from my arms to be placed in the arms of the parents who had prayed so long and so hard for him. We met them too. What a blessing, what an unbelievable story (one of so many we would be part of in the future)!

I had such joy for this new family, but an indescribable grief that I could not even begin to understand or process. There was such a paradox between my elation for this beautiful family that only a loving Heavenly Father could create, and the devastating loss I felt when I thought of never being able to rock, or kiss, or hold my little "son" again. I wasn't prepared for these feelings!

We took him home for one more night while his parents

prepared for his entry into their home. How I cherished every minute of that night! And so began a ritual for me that continues today, more than fifteen years later…the last night, the last bath, the last song, the last bottle. The next morning, our entire family dressed up and went to the agency to take our baby to the placement ceremony. How would I explain this to my children, ages six, three, and two? Would they understand? How would this affect their lives? As I placed Christopher in his mother's arms, my entire being changed in a way I was not expecting. I kissed him, smiled and left in a puddle of tears, assuring the agency I would be fine.

But I wasn't fine. In fact, I was anything but fine. For three days, I wept. The emptiness was beyond compare. The grief was remarkable. The despair could not be explained. I couldn't even look at pictures of him without an excruciating sense of loss. After seeing the "It's a Boy!" sign in his new family's yard, I cried to the Lord, "I cannot take this! I cannot do this!" Finally, on day three, I woke up and whispered to the Lord, "I have a family, Father, that I've got to take care of. Please, please help me get through this."

God is faithful. He took my grief and began the process of teaching me life lessons about the call He had placed on my heart. These were lessons that would be repeated again and again and are still being repeated to me today, as my stubborn and selfish heart sometimes refuses to learn. Lesson number one: Doing God's work is not easy. I love fun and games! I love for people to be happy. I am, by nature, an optimistic people pleaser. But, life is not always fun and games. He did not promise me, when He called me to be a foster mom, that there would be no pain, no grief, no sacrifice. Lesson number two: Along with other things, grief is part of the sacrifice I present to Him every time I embrace a baby for the first time. In 1 Chronicles 21 an angel of the Lord told David to build an altar on the threshing floor of a man named Ornan. Ornan offered to give the threshing floor, the animal, and all of the supplies for the burnt offering to David. But David realized that it would not be his offering if it cost him nothing: "No, but I will surely buy it for the full price; for I will not take what is yours for the Lord, or offer a burnt offering which costs me nothing." (1 Chronicles 21:24) Foster care costs. And lesson number three: If I did not love each baby/child, from the minute I touch him/her, as if they are my own, with total abandon, with my whole heart and soul, God would not have called me to this ministry. These children don't need a mother who is detached; they have already experienced loss. They need a mother who will throw open her heart, throw open her arms and embrace them with a love that changes everyone and everything it touches. Heavenly Father, let that be me.

What a Difference a "Day" Makes!

CHAPTER THREE

Our son, Connor, was born in March of the next year. What a joy and blessing he was and is to our family! I know it may be hard to understand, but even with my own newborn son in my arms, my heart ached to continue the ministry that had become such an important part of my life. As fall arrived that year, I grew increasingly frustrated with the fact that I didn't think the agency would allow us to care for an infant when we already had one. As I would pray, I'd tell the Lord that I knew on my own I couldn't care for two babies, but I believed that with His help, I could. One Sunday morning in October as I sat in my Sunday school class, the teacher made a comment about committing ourselves to ministry. I didn't realize that my internal sigh made an external noise! The teacher, who knew me very well, looked over and said, "Why are you sighing? Your foster care ministry is a great one." What she didn't know was that I was sighing because I felt useless at the time; the deepest part of me was unfulfilled because I was unable to do what I felt called to do.

The next morning as I read my Bible, I came across a passage that would change me forever. It said, "Do not withhold good from those to whom it is due, when it is in your power to do it." (Proverbs 3:27) I said out loud to the Lord, "That is exactly what I mean, Father! When You empower me, it is in my power to do this."

At noon the telephone rang. It was the pregnancy counselor at the agency. I began crying before she even told me why she called. She told me that she had a "situation" and that I should hear her out before I said yes or no. She went on to explain that there was a birth mother whom they had worked with two years earlier. She had wanted to make an adoption plan for her now two-year-old son, but for some reason did not. Now, she was ready; she just couldn't handle the pressure any more. "Okay," I thought, "this wasn't exactly what I had in mind." After all, we were used to newborns. But I knew in my heart that this was exactly what God had been preparing me for earlier in the day.

"We need a home for him," the counselor said.

"You've got one," I replied.

And so began an incredible chapter in the life of a little boy that I'll call "Day." He arrived at our home later in the day, straight from his birth mother to us. Honestly, we expected the worst and we prayed for the best.

Day came into our home and into our hearts like a soft gentle breeze. He was beautiful, well cared for, and ready to fall into our family routine. We knew very little about him, so we just did what parents do. We didn't know if he was used to a baby bed or a "big boy bed" so we put him on a pallet on our bedroom floor. During the first night he cried out, so I comforted him, patted him and got him back to sleep. Later in the night when he cried out again, Jeff put him in bed between us. As he lay there in a sleepy haze he said in a soft raspy voice, "Where Mama?" Jeff and I were silent. We were broken. Neither of us would ever forget that moment. We wanted to tightly embrace our new little son and let him know that even though things would never be the same, he would be all right. And that's exactly what we did.

By noon the next day he was following Cara, yelling, "Daddy! Daddy!" when Jeff came home for lunch. He never looked back. He truly was a gift.

A family was found for him immediately and after the ten day wait, it was time for him to leave. I was not prepared. I knew in my heart that it would be harder on him if Jeff and I took him to the placement, and I didn't want him to think that every mother he had known in his short life was going to leave him, so I opted not to go. As I gathered his things and prepared him to leave, he sensed that something was different. When we put him in the caseworker's car along with his belongings, he began to cry and cry and cry, "Mama! Mama!" I kissed him one last time and as the car drove away, I stood in the driveway — empty, motionless, heartsick.

Day's time in our home was another lesson to me about God's ability to accomplish His will in and through me. I basked in the wonder of God answering my prayer in such a tangible perfect way. Once again, He affirmed my call to serve as a mom-in-the-middle and His timing was flawless!

Bits and Pieces

CHAPTER FOUR

One spring we had a baby boy that our daughter Cara named Phillip after her best friend at the time. We knew we would only have Phillip for ten days, and I was prepared for that. What I wasn't prepared for was what God showed me at his placement service. I had been more burdened than usual for his birth mother and more impressed to pray diligently for her (even though I knew very little about her). When I arrived at the placement, the pregnancy counselor gave me a large box and told me that Phillip's birth mother had sent an outfit for him to meet his forever family in. As the counselor left the room, I sat down alone to dress our boy. I opened the box, and glimpsed a snapshot of this mother's sweet heart and deep love for her son:

a teddy bear, a quilt, a precious little outfit and a sterling silver cup engraved for her son as a reminder of how much she loved him. As I held him close and wept, I felt his mother's pain. I sensed her unconditional love — a love that threw away selfish desires, and went so deep it was willing to let go. With tears in my eyes and a love in my heart for a young woman I will never meet, I presented baby Phillip to his forever family. Lord, never let me forget that moment.

Baby Daniel…as I type those two words such a sense of peace comes over me. Baby Daniel. Our son Caleb named him after his best friend. He was our first bi-racial son and a gorgeous little guy. I will never forget the first bath I gave him. After I bathed him and washed his straight black hair, I put a hooded towel over him and went to lotion him up and get him dressed. When I took the towel off, he had the most beautiful black ringlets I had ever seen!

He was a gentle, easy going baby: calm, cool, and collected. He was a snuggler, a baby lover's dream. He spent six weeks with us. I treasured every day as I held him and sang to him and talked to him. I told him stories, especially about Daniel in the Bible; and just as God had a plan for that Daniel's life, He had a plan for our Daniel. When I knew his time for leaving was drawing near, I prayed he wouldn't smile. But he did. This was to be another learning experience for me. We had never had a baby that long, and although now six weeks seems like an instant, back then it was an eternity!

The day I dreaded came. I heard the voice on the other end say that the attorney for the agency had given them clearance for Daniel to join his forever family. Although that was great news in the midst of the legal battle the agency was in, I felt as if I had been hit in the stomach by a world-class boxer. It was that intense. It was excruciating. I held him close and began the ritual of gathering his things, buying a gift for his family, and jotting down some notes about his care.

Even as I type this, it's difficult to explain the grief that comes with foster care when there should be, and is, so much joy as a new little family is formed. You are caught between what you know is a God-blessed union between this precious baby and his parents, and the selfishness of not wanting the relationship you have with this child to end. As I said, it's unexplainable.

When we met Daniel's parents, we were once again struck with the intricacies of God's plan for the lives of these children. He does not leave anything undone. In Daniel's case, his parents lived near some of our best friends, and our friends knew them well. Quite honestly, at first it was hard to hear them talk about seeing Daniel and holding him. Nevertheless, we would have the joy of being able to keep in touch with him and watch him grow. How good God is to put aside my selfish desires, to excuse my selfish intentions and allow me the privilege to see His hand! The experience with Baby Daniel was a canvas on which the Lord would begin a masterpiece that is still a work in progress today, and for that I am immeasurably grateful.

Baby Blake, I get sleepy just saying his name! He was the biggest challenge we had faced up to that time. To say he had his days and nights mixed up would be a phenomenal understatement! I didn't know which way was up and which way was down; I was in a fog. He was discontented, unhappy, colicky, and was just genuinely a difficult baby. He was in our home for seven weeks, but it felt like forever! (I say that with great love and affection.) I may have been exhausted at the time, but not too exhausted to learn an important lesson from the Lord. One day, He brought to my mind the Scripture about the "least of these." I looked at Blake, a tiny, unhappy baby boy with no waiting family, and realized that he embodied this Scripture. He was "the least of these," and no matter how I felt at the time, it was my job to be Jesus to him. What a joy it was to see God provide the perfect forever family for this very important little guy, a sleepy family, but the perfect forever family!

Baby Keesha was a beautiful but stoic baby girl. I don't think I have ever seen a baby that enjoyed smiling any less than Keesha did. She was easy-going. She was not unhappy, but if she was happy, she didn't let it show! An interesting thing happened to me while she was in our home. I was on my way to church one Wednesday night and decided to make a quick trip to The Gap to see if there was anything we couldn't live without. I hurried into the mall, found a cute outfit on the sale rack and got in line. As I stood in line, standing next to me was a woman with a toddler in a stroller. I felt her eyes scanning me and the precious little one I had in the infant seat beside me. I hate to say it, but I thought the worst: "She's wondering why I have an African American baby; she wonders what my story is, and she doesn't approve." She continued staring and I smiled, but there was no responding smile from her. She made her purchase. I was next. As I placed my outfit on the counter, an unbelievable thing happened. She put her credit card down and told the clerk to charge my purchase to her account. I was stunned and blessed at the same time. I instinctively reached out to her and hugged her. (At this point I could tell that she, on the other hand, was not a hugger!) But, as I told her how grateful I was for her kindness, I looked into her tearful eyes and saw her pain. I don't know what the source of the pain was, but it was there, nonetheless — and for some reason on that particular night, her relief came through blessing me and Keesha. Wherever this woman is today, I pray that God has taken whatever anguish that was in her life and turned it into triumph. I pray that along the way she has been blessed like she blessed me during our not-by-chance encounter in such an unlikely place!

Yes, we've had twins too! Joshua and Rachel, the "Twinkies," were preemies that came to our home from another foster family at the age of seven weeks. They were on all sorts of medication and both wore heart monitors. As I think about them, I realize that I don't really remember too much about their stay! Jeff and I laughed so much during that time. I don't know if the laughter was out of sheer exhaustion or the fact that every time we turned around we were getting tangled up in the cords from the heart monitors! Both of us would work to get them to sleep at night. I would always accuse Jeff of picking out the sleepiest one and getting him/her to bed, so that by the time I got mine to sleep the other one would be awake! It was an experience that I wouldn't trade for anything, but one that I wouldn't want to repeat too often. A family from another state was chosen for them and we were excited to learn they were a childless couple who would now have a ready-made family. When we met them, we were elated. Joshua looked just like his new dad, and seeing their new daddy hold them in his huge hands was like viewing a work of art. The neatest part of their story is that this couple hadn't told their family members they were adopting twins, just that they were going out of state to pick up their baby. What I wouldn't have given to have been there for the intense joy that followed them off the airplane and into the arms of their families — as they **each** had a baby cradled in their arms! A few years later, they stopped through our city and visited us. It was another incredible story of the intricacies of God's family-building plan.

Just in the Nick of Time

*S*erving the Lord and convenience do not often go hand in hand. Sometimes I think God smiles as He calls us to serve when our plate is already too full of so many things we call important — things that tie us to "busy-ness" and leave us little freedom to fulfill our calling, our destiny. One such time was the day I got the call about Nick. I was heading up a group of women who were decorating, cooking, serving, and entertaining for an important evaluation team at my children's elementary school. I was up to my ears in chocolate pies when the call came. I had made the decision early on in this ministry that I would not say no to a placement unless I had a sick child. I knew that God's timing was so much better than mine. And as usual, in the case of Nick, God's timing was impeccable, whether I was aware of it at the time or not.

We got the call the day before Nick was to be released from the hospital, so we had time to contemplate a name for him. I made a list of boys' names that I liked and took it before the kids. They each had a favorite, but since it was my turn I cast the deciding vote: Nicholas.

I went to the agency to pick up our new little son. He was beautiful. (Have I said that about every baby to this point?) Well, he was. I loaded him up in the car seat and we began a journey together that would transform all of our lives.

Our family and Nick bonded quickly. It just felt right. Connor would lie beside Nick and rub his forearms over Nick's soft hair, an action that seemed to comfort them both. There was not a waiting family for Nick, so we knew we would have some additional time with him. What we didn't know was how much time, and what an impact this little man would have on our lives. He traveled with us on vacation and spent endless hours at the baseball park. He just "fit." As families for him came to the forefront and then fell through, we wrestled about whether or not we were supposed to adopt him. I honestly could not imagine our lives without him, but deep down inside, I had an unsettling feeling, no peace.

After months of prayer and questioning God's will for us and for "our son," I got a call from the agency. As usual, they were in tune with my feelings and asked me once again if we were sure Nick was not to be our forever son. With much sadness, I told them that we had no confirmation. They proceeded to tell me about a family from another state that had already adopted three children and were very interested in Nick. There is no way to explain the feeling I had when I heard those words. It was as if all the air had been sucked out of my lungs.

A few days later, with my permission, this adoptive mom called to talk with me about Nick. Remarkably, I made it through the entire conversation with my tear ducts intact, but when the receiver hit the base, I hit the kitchen countertop. Oblivious to what was going on around me, I threw myself down and began to weep. I was in my own little world of grief until I felt a little hand pulling on my leg. It was the hand of my then two-year-old son, Connor. I noticed he disappeared for a minute and then felt his hand there again. When I looked down, I saw God's provision for my need in the form of an unwrapped Band-Aid with Neosporin ointment neatly placed on the little gauze pad. A little chubby two-year-old hand reached out to me with the hand of God to cover my pain. That little two-year-old did the only thing he knew to do to help Mommy's "boo-boo" get better. I took the Band-Aid, grease and all, and stuck it to my journal where it still is today. God taught me an incredible lesson with my son's simple gesture: He can and will meet my needs using whatever and whomever He chooses. God understood my grief and would cover me with His choice of Band-Aids.

Not long after that, the time came for Nick to leave us. I wish I could say I handled the transition gracefully, but honestly, it was a very difficult time. If I hadn't always been so totally sure of God's call on my life to do foster care, this would have been one of the times I would have thrown up my hands and screamed, "Why in the world am I putting myself through this?" I think my words at the time say it best. Here is the note exactly as I wrote it in my journal the night before Nick left us:

If we had desired to adopt Nick, it would be a done deal. We battled with this. In all my selfishness I've screamed inside NO ONE IS GOING TO TAKE MY SON AWAY! And yet, I have never felt a peace about adopting him. I've read passages about Moses' mother and I feel a distant kinship with her. Tomorrow is the day that our little son makes his way to his permanent family. How I pray that God will give me the strength to make it through!

The next day we loaded up our boy, his things, and our hearts and made our way to the agency's office. We were in the parking lot taking a few last-minute pictures when we saw a family get out of a van. They looked our direction and headed into the building. It was excruciating knowing that Nick would leave in that van and I would leave once again with an empty car seat and a heavy heart. We made our way into the office.

As I met Nick's forever family, I was strangely comforted. I knew then why we had not felt a peace about adopting him. This was his family. It was obvious. His adoptive mother was so gentle with him and with me. She understood my deep love for my son, her son. It was if she saw straight through to my soul and was able to tangibly touch that part of me. What a sweet placement service we had that day! God carried me through in a way I never would have thought possible. He allowed me to release something, someone so precious to me, with the assurance that it was His perfect will in His perfect time. A picture that was taken at the placement spoke volumes about the intensity of the day: Nick was in the arms of his new mother — holding on to my hand.

And he would always have hold of my hand, even today.

We have kept in touch with Nick and his family. Five years after he left us, his parents called to ask if we would be willing to have him come and stay with us for two weeks while they finalized an adoption in another country. We jumped at

CHAPTER 5: *Just in the Nick of Time*

the chance, yet wondered how Nick would feel staying with "strangers." I got my answer at the airport when I flew to pick him up. He ran across the terminal and jumped into my arms! It was an amazing moment and one I will never forget. I thought, "His mom has put him up to this to make me feel better." But when I talked with her later that evening after we had both returned home, she said, "We knew he would be all right when we saw how he greeted you." She had nothing to do with his welcoming me; somewhere deep within he knew me. Jeff commented throughout the two weeks that Nick and I shared such a special connection, a supernatural one. I honestly expect to open my front door one day to a handsome godly man raised by the forever family that God ordained, coming to visit the "middle" family that God ordained for a special time.

Alex
Uncharted Waters

CHAPTER SIX

*O*ne fall, we had a short-term baby named Faith who left us unexpectedly. It's hard to explain, but those were frustrating times when a baby would come into our home and our lives and then suddenly be whisked back to the birth mother. Right after this particular baby left, I remember praying as I drove along one day that the Lord would not allow so much time to pass between opportunities to minister. I got a call that week about a baby, a baby who would alter the course of my life and ministry in a remarkable way.

His name was Alex. Alex was not typical of the babies who came to our house. They were usually newborns, one to two-days old. Alex was the five-month-old son of a teenage birth mother with two other children. She had wanted to make an adoption plan for him at birth but was talked out of it by well-meaning family members who promised to help. After five months and no help, she was desperate. She was trying to go to school, work and care for three children, and she was not succeeding. She called the agency and they called me. I still remember picking Alex up at the agency. Of course, he was beautiful, but there was something so hopeless about him. He was sad, listless, and unemotional. Even at his age, he seemed depressed, neglected and afraid to make eye contact. His skin was ashen and his eyes sunken. From the moment I laid eyes on him, I loved him. I took him in my arms and into my heart. I wanted him to know his life would never be the same; God had his destiny in His hands! Our family set out to be God's hands, God's voice, and God's love to this little guy who needed it so much.

Alex and I dropped by the agency about a week later, and as the staff greeted us, they gasped at the incredible transformation that one week and a ton of love had caused. Our "son" was smiling, his skin was no longer ashen, and we were all beginning to comprehend the vast difference that unconditional love and affection can make! The birth-parent counselor put it like this:

"In the twinkling of an eye, Alex's whole world changed. That first day he looked so frightened, a small black face in a house full of white people. His skin had no sheen to it, his hair was thin, his eyes full of wonder. It was not wonder like a child at Disney World or a child seeing Christmas lights and Santa for the first time, but a wonder of what had just happened to him and the life he had known, however ne-

glected he might have been. Over the next five days, we saw a little boy who was still overwhelmed by the attention, but now had a smooth and healthy sheen to his skin. His eyes were still full of wonder, but now the wonder was of the world around him and the understanding that it might be an all right place to be. There was even a smile that would come across his face when he saw our eyes and heard our voices and felt our unconditional love. It was so obvious. Now that he was being loved, nurtured, and cared for, it was written all over him, it showed!"

As I contemplated Alex's situation, the Lord began to reveal some truths to me. It seems that so many times we as Christians focus so heavily on the sin that we forget the sinner. An unmarried woman's unplanned pregnancy is a placard that announces to the world that a sin has been committed. What if we all wore placards that listed our sins so overtly? We are so critical of young women with unplanned pregnancies and especially with those who have multiple pregnancies outside of marriage. I have heard so many people make judgmental comments like "Why do they keep having babies? Why don't they have their tubes tied? Why are we having to pay for all of these babies?" The Lord spoke to me in a quiet voice and said, "Christie, it's not your job to assess the situation to be critical and judge; it is your job to be Jesus to this hurting and hopeless young mother and her son." As a child of the King, I owed Alex something; I owed his birth mother something. Wow! What a concept — don't judge, be Jesus. With that concept planted in my heart, I set out on my mission to be Jesus to Alex. And even though I would never meet his mother, I prayed that she knew there was another mother who loved her and her son, and who was asking the heavenly Father to intervene on her behalf.

Alex was so much fun! Since he was not a newborn, he could relate to us, smile and laugh at us, communicate with us. We all loved it, and him! We prayed that the Lord would provide him with the perfect family who would continue to allow him to blossom and reach his full potential. That is exactly what happened. The answer was wonderful, but the timing (to my taste) was terrible. He left us and joined his forever family three days before Christmas. He would be an only son. What a gift, an only son, three days before the celebration of the birth of the Ultimate Only Son! As we met his family, we rejoiced for Alex and we celebrated the choice of a desperate young mother who, in her desperation, gave her son the ultimate gift.

In the days following Alex's departure, the Lord began once again to move in my heart and life. As I thought about his birth mother, I thought about all the other birth mothers who take their babies home from the hospital and then realize a month, six months, or a year down the road that they made the wrong decision about parenting. I thought about how many of those birth mothers eventually give in to frustration, exhaustion and despair only to abuse or neglect their children and lose them to the custody of the state. How could I help them? How could I intervene to ensure that babies like Alex had a chance at life as it was designed to be? Could God use me, just one person, to help these mothers? Those were questions that had no easy answers. I began to pray. I began to seek and to soul-search and to reach deep within myself. There had to be an answer. As the months wore on, I found myself stealing away more and more to seek the Lord, to find out what was next.

This was a time, honestly, when I wished the Lord would just send the next step to me in the form of an instruction booklet that floated down from heaven and landed in my lap. But that is not the way He works, is it? And it was an impatient time. "Lord, can't you just tell me what to do, so that I can get a move on? Time is "a-wastin'!" This was to be a long, arduous process. But I'll get to that later.

Alexa
Hope Renewed

About nine months after Alex left, I got a call about Alexa. Just thinking about Alexa puts a smile on my face. You see, she is a miracle. She is a living, breathing, beautiful example of God's intervention in the life of a child that the world seemed to think was disposable. Boy, were they wrong.

Alexa was born with Down syndrome. And because of that, she was abandoned at birth by parents who just couldn't handle the fact that their child was "imperfect."

When we got the call, I related to the agency's director that we had some dear friends who, years before, had a vivacious engaging and precious son named, Joshua, who, by the way, also had Down syndrome. Joshua's parents had been (and still are) a powerful example of taking what some might call a tragic turn of events and embracing it with all they had: all the love, all the joy, all the humor, all the energy and all the praise in order to point people to the One who never creates a mistake. Because of their example, many people who have lived through similar circumstances have triumphed just as they have, and their persistence and vigilance have made an impact far beyond their human understanding. Joshua is now a thriving, talented, gracious and godly twenty-two-year old young man!

I digress, back to Alexa. She was to be released from the hospital in two days, so we began preparations. Unfortunately, on the day she was to come home, she became violently ill. Not as a result of the Down syndrome, but with an unrelated intestinal problem. She might not make it. How could we get to her? We couldn't let this baby die alone.

The agency pleaded with the hospital staff to let us come be with her, but because we were not officially her legal guardians, that could not happen; not at *that* hospital. We asked our family and friends to pray. God intervened. Because of the severity of the situation, Alexa had to be transferred to another hospital's NICU…and *that* hospital's policy, well let's just say it was remarkably different. The social worker called me and said, "Mrs. Erwin, the way we see it is that you and Mr. Erwin are Alexa's parents, with all the rights and responsibilities as such — and you are welcome here any time to be with your daughter." That was all I needed to hear.

I raced to the hospital, relieved and terrified. I had no idea what to expect, or even how to act in this situation. As I made my way to the NICU, my heart told me to follow its lead. Just do what a mother does. As I looked down into the little isolette that held this tiny, pale little person with tubes coming out in every direction, doing what a mother does was not hard to do. This was my daughter, and at that moment the love in my heart overflowed. I bent down and told her I loved her, I touched her hand and rubbed my finger across her cheek. I knew right then that even though the medical staff had access to her whole story, no one in that hospital was going to walk away from my daughter thinking that just because she was abandoned, she was unimportant, "less than," or unwanted. With fiery determination, I made it my mission to ensure that her worth (both to us and to the heavenly Father) was known to anyone who would listen. That proved to be a very easy task, because everyone who came in contact with Alexa fell in love with her. And everyone who knew her story made it *their* mission to ensure her value.

She had a rough road ahead. We spent eleven weeks in the NICU. She had three surgeries. There were times we were not sure she would make it. There were times when she was so pale and her breathing so shallow. There were times when we questioned what God was going to do in her life. I am convinced we were surrounded by the most selfless, caring group of nurses ever to exist, and I was blessed beyond measure to be announced as "Alexa's Mom" every time I entered the unit. Her crib was decorated with pictures of our family, with crayon drawings our children had made, with lots and lots (and lots) of pink and with balloons; (I was even reprimanded by a stern charge nurse for having one balloon over the limit!)

I spent my time reading to Alexa, holding her, singing quietly, praying for her and rubbing her soft little head. I watched as babies came in, and I grieved as babies died. I saw parents from every walk of life, all with the same mission that I had: to leave the hospital with a healthy baby. As I look back, I realize it was a very intense time as I vacillated between caring for my family and sitting at the hospital off and on during NICU visiting hours, three times a day, but it was also a time of intense power. It was a time when God's hand was on my shoulder guiding every step I took. I knew that I was involved in something much bigger than myself, and I could feel the prayers of God's people.

The agency sent out the following newsletter during the time Alexa was hospitalized:

"For You formed my inward parts; You covered me in my mother's womb. I will praise You, for I am fearfully and wonderfully made; marvelous are Your works, and that my soul knows very well. My frame was not hidden from You, when I was made in secret, and skillfully wrought in the lowest parts of the earth. Your eyes saw my substance, being yet unformed. And in Your book they all were written, the days fashioned for me, when as yet there were none of them." Psalm 139:13-16 NKJV

"Her name is Alexa. She was born not long ago, a tiny little one. Packaged in a special way, we know that she has Down syndrome and some other health related issues. She has been placed in our care for the purpose of adoption. However, she is still in the hospital fighting for her life. Until she is well and able to leave the hospital, her foster family and the staff visit her every day, often three times a day. We have no doubt she is being held in the strong arms of Jesus. We know that He has a plan for her and

we consider it a wonderful privilege to be a part of His plan as we watch it unfold. We stare at her and know that we will defend her and protect her as long as we are called to do so. Looking at Alexa, we don't know who God has called her to be and how He will use her. We do know, however, that God has a hope and a future for her. We know that God formed her, that her frame was not hidden from Him, and that no matter how she looks to the world and how they see her potential, she is fearfully and wonderfully made! We are resolved to seek God's perfect family for her. We have faith that even now, God is designing and preparing them, whoever they may be, as we fervently pray that He will anoint them with abundant love and compassion. We pray He will open doors and that He will move mountains so that He can use her in every way He desires. Our ultimate prayer for Alexa is that she will come to know the Lord as her personal Savior, and that her life, as we already see that it is, will bring Him great glory!"

After eleven weeks, Alexa got to go home! We left with a great fanfare from the hospital staff and with great joy in our hearts for this precious little girl who had impacted so many lives! Alexa had lots of health issues that kept us at home and away from as many 'germs' as possible. She had been through so much, and yet she was so calm, so patient, so loving. There was no family waiting for her, and we silently wondered who they would be. My heart ached at the thought of her ever leaving me. As I had done a few times before when a baby was waiting for a family, I began to pray and ask the Lord if Alexa was to be our daughter forever. Although I had experienced the loss many times, I could not imagine our lives without her.

We continued to pray, but God held back His answer, that is until one night as I was getting ready for bed. As I was washing my face and brushing my teeth, I found myself in deep thought and began praying out loud. I remember it as if it were yesterday.

I said, "Lord, is Alexa supposed to be our daughter forever?"

And with profound clarity the Lord whispered to me, "Christie, I can't do what I want to do in you and through you if you adopt Alexa."

With the frustration of an unhappy child, I said out loud "Well, then it better be something spectacular, because I cannot let her go."

I have to say I didn't stop hoping or praying that I wasn't just going to be Alexa's middle mom, but I knew from that moment on that God had a remarkable plan for her life and that our place in that plan was temporary.

Two months after her release from the hospital, we returned by ambulance with terrible respiratory problems. During the two weeks we were there, the agency got a call from a woman who wanted to help me in some way. Her name was Jill. They asked me if I would allow her to sit with Alexa for a couple of hours while I went home to freshen up and rest. I reluctantly agreed. However, when Jill arrived, it was if we had known each other for our entire lives. She seemed so much like me, and she was smitten with Alexa. As I left the hospital for that short respite, I remember thinking to myself, "I may have just met Alexa's mother."

And I had. This family had already added a child from

another country to their biological family. I would learn later that Jill had always wanted to adopt a child with Down syndrome. After she left the hospital, Jill called the agency and inquired about whether or not there was a family for Alexa. They began the process, and a month later, Alexa became their daughter.

I remembered that night of prayer in my bathroom. I remembered saying, "Spectacular!" and then I thought about Jill and her family. God had not only given my Alexa the most perfect family in the world for her, but He had given me a lifelong friend. Where my emotions were concerned, Jill embodied the word empathy. She seemed to have a supernatural understanding about the foster care process and what it was like to lose a child you loved so much and had cared for so long. Her love and mercy on me made this transition so sweet.

Sometime later, their family moved to another state. And now years later, when Jill and I talk, it's as if we talk every day! Alexa is a healthy beautiful girl who is loved beyond measure by the family that God ordained just for her!

The Alex Project
A Vision Originates

*D*uring our time with Alexa, the Lord was continuing to stir my heart regarding Alex and his situation. I thought about Alex often and wondered how many other children, like him, needed to be rescued from birth parents that were overwhelmed, overextended and on the verge of doing something irrational. I continued praying and seeking God's plan during the time we were caring for Alexa. Some interesting things happened too. One day, as I drove to the hospital, I was praying out loud about what God wanted me to do, what new step He wanted me to take. I found myself saying "Bless this Alex project." I knew right then that whatever "it" was, it was to be called The Alex Project.

And the confirmation of that just kept coming. First of all, there was a doctor that I became friends with in the NICU. She was pregnant at the time and had her baby during our stay.

She named her baby Alex.

When we returned to the hospital two months after we were released, we were put in a semi-private room with a young mother and her son. You guessed it, Alex. This was not just a confirmation…it was a CONFIRMATION! We had ridden by ambulance to the hospital, waited forever in the emergency room, and then were whisked to a room, a semi-private room. I was worn out. I was worried about my baby. Frankly, the last thing I wanted to do was minister. Just as I got Alexa settled in, it began. The young mother in the room we shared began a long night of frustration with a sick one-year-old. She yelled, she swatted, she sighed; she left for a smoke. I fumed. I sulked. I sighed. (No, I didn't leave for a smoke!) Both of the babies were in isolation. On one of this mom's smoke breaks, her son began to cry and cry. Alexa slept quietly. My soul was moved, and so I went to him. I patted him, sang to him and reassured him that his mommy would return soon. But I was back in my seat when she returned. Boy, did she need an attitude adjustment!

I would soon find out, it was really me who needed the attitude adjustment.

My mom came the next day to give me some much needed respite. As I made my way home, the Lord began to speak to me. He reminded me of what He had told me months before about my Alex; that I was not to judge, I was to be Jesus to a helpless, hurting young mother and her son; that as a child of God I owed her something, I owed Alex something! And now, here I was with another young mother and another little guy named Alex. And once again, it was not my job to judge; it was my job to be Jesus to a hurting young mother and her son. In humility, my heart broke as I contemplated my selfishness, my frustration, my impatience, my lack of concern and my impiety.

Who did I think I was? I confessed these things to the Lord and committed to be whatever He wanted me to be to this mother.

My attitude towards this young mother changed immediately. When I returned to the hospital, I was a changed woman. I began to listen as she recounted her life's story. She was not married to Alex's father and had no support from him of any kind; in fact, it had been six months since he had seen his son. She had no support from anyone. As I heard her words, I understood her actions. And as I put myself in her place, I realized that I would be yelling, swatting, sighing and probably smoking too!

Then something else happened. I began to love her. Deep down in my heart, I felt her pain. As I left the hospital again, she asked if I could get her a book of crosswords. I got her the crosswords and I got her a copy of THE Word. I could not believe the change that God had brought in me. I wanted to make life easier for this mother. I wanted to do anything that would ease the burden she was carrying. Suddenly, the Lord took me from my own "pity party" to a place of genuine joy as I reached out with His hands to this soul who needed Him so desperately.

In a day or two, we were moved to a private room. I felt both relief and a sense of sadness. The next day when this young mother readied Alex to be discharged from the hospital, she sought me out. She wanted to thank me for the gifts. As we talked further, I realized a financial need that the Lord wanted to meet through me. When I mentioned to her that Jeff and I would like to help her in that way, she threw her arms around me and squeezed me as if she had known me for years. With tears in her eyes, she left the hospital, and I realized that so many times I miss the blessing of ministry because I am too tired, too selfish, and too stubborn to hear from the Father. I can't remember this young woman's name and will likely never see her again, but I pray that God will never let me forget her and never let me forget the attitude adjustment that changed my life.

After Alexa left us, a long ministry dry spell began. It seemed that the more I searched for what The Alex Project would be, the fewer opportunities I had to minister to babies in our state. The staff at the agency was definitely on board. They were incredible encouragers and offered to do whatever they could to help me. Our friends donated money to get The Alex Project off the ground; we had a logo designed, bought stationery, had business cards printed and sent out loads of information. The scope of the vision became crystal clear to me: 1) Help-for birth mothers who found themselves with an unplanned pregnancy and wanted to make an adoption plan, 2) Hope-for birth mothers who had taken their babies home to parent and realize later that they made the wrong decision and 3) Healing-for babies/children who were unwanted, abused or neglected.

God allowed me to cast the vision He had given me to many different individuals and groups. For the most part, people agreed that there needed to be help, hope and healing for children and birth parents in our state. But, the more I cast, the less I caught! Nothing tangible seemed to be happening. No babies were coming our way. In fact, we had never had so many months without being able to minister to a foster child. It didn't seem like we were reaching the birth mothers or babies we were so passionate about reaching. What was going on?

God's plan was going on. And though it would be months and even years before I saw what He had in mind for me, He knew. He was working above and beyond what my finite mind could understand. About this time, some money was donated to The Alex Project. As I talked with the agency about how best to use this money to get the word out, we decided that billboards were an advertising avenue we hadn't tried yet. This decision would be another opportunity for the Father to show the intricacies of His power.

I had purchased a print, from an online art site, of a baby looking out over her crib. It was gripping, and in my mind I could see that precious, innocent face on billboards all over our city. There was just one problem: How would I get permission to use it from an artist I had never heard of, and had no idea where he lived? Well, that small detail wasn't enough to keep me down! I began calling art gallery after art gallery; no one had a clue. Finally, after many calls, a voice on the other end was the artist, Tim Hinton. He listened intently as I told my story, presented my passion and asked the question, "Could I use the picture on a billboard (of all things)?"

He told me about his art, about his long career and the many honors he had received in the field of art. He was so humble and so engaging. I realized as I talked with him that this was an important man who knew important people and had had his art exhibited in important places! He was not only listening; he was hearing. He heard my heart and gave me his permission to use the picture any way I wanted. I was amazed. I was elated! I couldn't believe what I had just heard. The next day a package arrived for me. It was a large, autographed copy of the print I loved so much, sent overnight by this artist-it was an exclamation point to the conversation the day before. It hangs in a prominent place in my living room today, a constant reminder that God is in the business of doing incredible things.

During this time, my friend Donna encouraged me with a Scripture about the vision that "tarries" in Habakkuk. When I went to my old Bible from my teenage years and read the verse, my mouth dropped open. It said "And the Lord said to me, 'Write my answer on a billboard, large and clear, so that anyone can read it at a glance and rush to tell the others. But these things I plan won't happen right away. Slowly, steadily, surely, the time approaches when the vision will be fulfilled. If it seems slow, do not despair, for these things will surely come to pass. Just be patient! They will not be overdue a single day!'" Habakkuk 2:2-3 (The Way, The Living Bible). And by the way, the billboards were unbelievable.

Shortly after the billboards went up, the agency began getting calls, mostly from parents wanting to adopt. But one day they received a call from a young woman who had taken a different route home than usual and had seen one of our billboards. Because of the billboard, she decided to make an adoption plan for her daughter. I was overwhelmed with joy, but I must admit that my heart sank, because another foster family got the privilege of caring for my "billboard baby": Baby Ella. That was a selfish bout of jealousy on my part! But an interesting thing happened; Baby Ella wasn't placed with her forever family as quickly as the agency thought, and the other foster family was leaving town on a three-week vacation. We got the call. Could we care for baby Ella? Here's the rest of the story as I wrote it in my journal several years ago:

We really thought that she (Ella) would be placed with her forever family within ten days or so, but in God's providence, she has been with us eight weeks. She is one of the most (if not the most) beautiful babies I have ever seen...with soft features, big eyes, and gorgeous soft curly hair (which always has a bow in it), I have had more comments about her from people than any other baby we have had. She has not been a real contented baby, in fact, she has screamed every time she has been in the car seat! I mean SCREAMED! She is my girl — a real momma's girl. She loves to snuggle up under my neck and sleep and she is usually so quiet when I hold her (which is all the time). She knows my voice and follows me with her eyes. She has a beautiful smile and seems to really carry on a conversation with me! When I took Ella to get her picture made this afternoon, I was praying about her situation. It's times like these when foster moms ask, "Why am I doing this again? Why do I continue to put myself through this terrible grief?" As I have thought about those questions over the past few days, I know the answers as I have always known the answers, God has called me to do this. He has not called me to begin this process as a birth mom, or to end this process as an adoptive mom, but He has called me to the middle; to take this precious one as my own for a season. I told the Lord that I didn't feel like it was right to pray that He would allow me to get through this with ease, but that He would allow me to get through this with grace. I really believe that the grief is part of the sacrifice that I must make in order to do His will. Honestly, it's the part I hate, watching someone else welcome "my baby" into their arms. That sounds terrible, and only a foster mom who has been through this would understand! There is incredible joy, knowing that God has ordained and called a family to embrace this child, there is a tremendous sense of awe at God's plan and His power to fulfill that plan, and yet there is sorrow, grief, and loss as I lose someone I love intensely and have bonded to in ways that can't be explained. I am thankful that I have a Heavenly Father who understands on a much larger scale what it is like to "give up a child." I pray tonight that God will give me the grace to let Ella go, knowing that nothing can take away the eight weeks she has been my "daughter" and the fact that I have poured myself into her, and she has poured herself into me. My life is so much more enriched for having had her in my life and for that I am truly grateful and humbled.

The Call, Part 2:
A Change of Venue

I began to think I had a hard head as the Lord once again confirmed The Alex Project to me. This time it was a waitress at a local drive in. (I have to admit, I still go there almost every day for a large Diet Coke with extra ice.) I had seen this girl several times and noticed she was pregnant. On one occasion, I asked when her baby was due. She seemed surprised that someone would even care. She told me her due date and what she planned to name her newborn son. I remembered the name because I have a nephew with the same name. Right after that, I bought a card for her with the good intentions of taking it by with some money in it for her before her baby was born. A few months later, the card was still in a pile in my kitchen, and I hadn't seen this young woman. One day, I dropped by the drive in for my "usual" on the way to a doctor's appointment. Guess who brought my drink out? It was the young woman, who was now a young mother. I knew this day was not left to chance. When she got to my car, I asked her how her baby was. Once again, she seemed surprised. She told me about her precious son and began to tell a story. During the story, she mimicked herself calling out to him at night "Alex!" I know she must have thought I was really strange from my expression.

"Alex?" I said.

"Yes, that is his name," she replied.

"I thought you were going to name him…" I retorted.

"I was, but I changed my mind," she responded matter-of-factly.

Alex. That was my cue. I rushed home, got the card, wrote a note, enclosed some cash and drove back to the drive-in. With all of the articulate speech I could muster, I called through the loud speaker, "Would you mind sending out the carhop with the baby boy named Alex?" They must not have thought I was too weird, because out she came.

I had never told her before about my heart for foster care, but that was about to change. I handed her the card. I told her that it had been sitting in my kitchen for several months, and that I felt like today God impressed me to give it to her. I told her how proud I was of her and her decision to give life to her son and to parent him. I told her about my life and the ministry that God had entrusted to me. And then, I handed her a business card with my name on it that also said "The Alex Project." She began to cry. She told me that she had been in foster care herself and recounted her bad experience. She hugged me and told me how much she appreciated my kindness. I told her that it wasn't me.

I ran into her a few times after that day. She always re-membered me and always talked about the day I brought the card to her. I wonder how many times I've left "cards in the kitchen" and missed an opportunity to be the hands of Jesus to someone who just needs to know He cares.

I refer to our foster care experience with the agency as the "country club of foster care." It was the crème de la crème of ministering in the foster care world. They were there for us. Empathy and sympathy reigned. They put themselves in our place. They laughed with us, cried with us, grieved with us. The pregnancy counselor at the agency would lovingly refer to foster moms as "last year's Miss Americas" because once a child was placed in the arms of his forever family, the foster mom faded off into the shadows (and rightly so); hence "last year's Miss America." We could even laugh together about that. They would write notes and give gifts. They would hug us and show such un-expected gratitude for our small part in the adoption process. It was as good as it could have been. In fact now I find it extremely amusing that I was so grief-stricken when our babies left us; for two-parent, godly Christian homes. What I wouldn't give for that now! If I went back today, I think my perspective would be very different.

However, as I mentioned earlier, God used our ministry dry spell as a conduit for change. It was a very difficult time, of searching deep within my soul for what I needed to do in order to continue to fulfill my calling. I loved the agency, I loved the staff; they were like family. But they needed fewer and fewer foster care placements because of the wonderful fact that babies were being placed with their forever families directly from the hospital. I don't ever think I would have made a move if babies had continued to come into my home and the Lord knew that.

Another problem was that at the agency, we were not able to meet the needs of children who were unwanted, abused, or neglected because those children had to be reported to the state and as a result, went into state custody.

As time went on and God continued to lead, the direction I was supposed to take became so clear. Finally, after much prayer and many internal battles about leaving versus staying, I knew what we had to do. It was time to move our ministry to the state. That was the only way The Alex Project could be realized completely. Although The Alex Project would no longer exist in name, it would be forever etched on the cornerstone of the new ministry God was leading me to build. And so a new journey began.

Serenity Now!

CHAPTER TEN

After we had completed our state foster care training classes, passed all of our background checks and home study, and been approved by the state, we began the wait. I knew that this was going to be a different experience — we "weren't in Kansas anymore." So my prayer for Jeff, because of the sacrifice he was willing to make, was that he would fall in love with the first baby or child that came into our home. Little did I know how prophetic that prayer would be.

About a month after our home opened, I received a call from a Department of Human Services, Division of Children and Family Services, supervisor about three siblings that had just come into care. She asked me what I thought. Although it is almost always in the best interest of the children to keep siblings together, I knew with our four biological children, we couldn't take all three. Due to the nature of this case, the caseworker decided that we would take the one-year-old and that our friends

Bill and Donna would take the three-year-old. There was a new-born that was expected to be in the hospital for awhile, so no immediate decision had to be made about him, (although he would eventually be placed with Bill and Donna as well).

The next day I talked with the placement coordinator and asked some basic questions: for example, what was this child's name? (That would be nice to know!) Her name was Serenity.

I grabbed my new car seat and a stuffed Glow-Worm that I had bought especially for this little girl and made my way to the DHS office. I have to admit it was frightening. With the agency, we knew what to expect; we knew the people and the process, but we were traversing new territory here, and I had no idea what lay ahead. (It's probably better that I didn't know!)

As I drove up, a caseworker let me in, and there in the arms of a big teenage boy (I would later learn was one of her brothers) was a precious sleeping little girl. I looked to the caseworker for instruction and cringed at the thought of taking this sleeping child from everything she had known to a world of uncertainty and very pale strangers! My heart broke as I tried to imagine what she was feeling. I took her in my arms and loaded her into the car seat. She awoke for a moment and looked at me with inquisitive eyes, but no tears.

Our first stop was The Gap! After all, I was used to new-borns, so my extensive infant wardrobe was too small. I had established a relationship over the years with Cindy at The Gap, and she was always so willing to help me and to encourage me. It was (and is) a pleasure to shop there. So, I hit the sale rack. Cindy helped me outfit Serenity, and our quest began!

Serenity was anything but Serene. She was a live wire that kept all of us hopping. She was beautiful and very precocious. It was as if she had a motor that never, ever ran out of gas. We did. It took all six of us to keep her under control and sometimes it felt like we were all tag-team wrestlers who took turns in the "ring"! But, she brought equally as much sheer joy as she brought activity. She was very loving. She was so curious and didn't want to miss anything. And she could get into some messes.

As she grew taller, she could get out the front door and did so every time she got the chance. This, of course, made us very nervous. So nervous, in fact, that when she was about two and a half, Jeff put a lock on the top of the door that everyone in our house could reach, except Serenity. After he installed it, we sat down in the family room to savor the victory of beating a toddler at her own game. Only, a minute or two later the doorbell rang. We went to the door, and guess who was standing there? Yes, the toddler who had outsmarted us! I guess she had taken Jeff's lock installation as the gauntlet being thrown down; she promptly unlocked and climbed out the window (which is low to the ground). Jeff immediately left for Home Depot, where he bought and installed window locks. Two can play this game. We won.

And speaking of locks... let's talk hair! For those of you who have never realized it, there is a difference between Caucasian hair and African American hair. Let me tell you firmly with conviction... there is a difference. I had taken care of the hair of African American babies, but now I was in new territory with an older child. I bought a book about the joys of keeping your African American daughter's hair natural. I bought products and more products, and more products. I stopped women in the ethnic hair aisle to ask their opinions, and let me say that no two opinions were the same! Everybody had an opinion about what needed to be done to Serenity's hair, and there seemed to be no direct or definitive answer. I wasn't ready for the hours of trying to detangle the hair of an extremely active toddler, not to mention the unusual hairstyles I would end up with. I wanted Serenity to be proud of her heritage, to celebrate who she was, not look like she had a Caucasian mother with no clue (and no ability to fix hair)! Someone told me that you would know you had reached the pinnacle of success when African American women stopped you and asked "Who did your little girl's hair?" Never happened. I took Serenity to several different salons, all with differing views on what needed to be done. It was an adventure to say the least. However, we finally found a hairdresser that felt my pain and encouraged me, and though I was far from an expert stylist, I'd come a long way, baby!

Serenity's case was very complicated. I don't feel that it would be appropriate or beneficial for me to be disrespectful of her birth family, the very people who provided the DNA for her life. Suffice it to say, though, that there were some real issues. The state's goal, as is usually the case, was for reunification. They wrote the case plan with that in mind, and those of us on the team began to implement that plan. There were visits between the children and their biological mother, doctor visits, therapy, drug screens, paternity tests, meetings with attorneys, developmental evaluations, psychological evaluations; all means to reach the end: reunification. But, the process is flawed. And we as people are flawed. Problems arose and crises came as time marched on — a lot of time.

Every time her birth mother stood on the precipice of success, success that would allow her to get her children back, something would cause her to stumble. It seemed she would subconsciously sabotage herself with drugs, missed appointments, overall apathy. It was sad. Yet, I found myself feeling guilty because deep inside, somewhere unspoken, I was secretly hoping she would fail. My love for Serenity and my desire to protect her became more important than any reunification effort, and it became more and more obvious that her birth mother was going to be anything but cooperative. The self absorbed nature of the drug culture makes it extremely difficult for a person immersed in that culture to put anyone or anything ahead of the next high, even one's own children.

On each visit and on every court date when I saw her birth mother, I wondered what she was thinking about me. How did it feel to have someone else mothering your child, to hear your child call someone else "Mommy?" As time wore on, I realized that she wasn't seeing the situation for what it was. I vacillated between outrage and empathy for a woman with whom I would never have a relationship. On one hand, I wanted to grab her by the shoulders and talk some sense into her, and on the other hand, I wanted to hug her and let her know there is a better way. Honestly, most of the time the desire to "grab" won out over the desire to "hug."

However, Serenity's birth mother did make some progress, enough to cause the powers that be to decide to send her children home for the weekend, with the hopes of sending them home for good after a trial period. In Serenity's life, nineteen months had gone by, which for a then two-year-old, was forever. Yet, she was expected to leave what she knew as "home" for a weekend with a family she really didn't know. Nevertheless, being a team player, I bought her a new duffle bag and packed her things. It was painful. I cried out to the Father to sustain all of us during this time. We had sung a praise song in church not long before with a line in it that says, "You give and take away." Could this really be God's will? Was He really going to take Serenity away from us? For me, the bottom line was would I trust Him if that was His will. I found myself praying all around the issue. Lord, take care of Serenity, protect her, bless her. I could never say I really wanted God's will for her, because I was too afraid of what that will would be. I was afraid it would mean that I would lose my daughter.

I couldn't wait to see Serenity on Sunday afternoon. I felt as if I had held my breath all weekend long. I finally exhaled as I wrapped my arms around her. She was home. But this was to be the beginning of the end of our relationship. She was going away forever and I was powerless to do anything about it. The next day, as I prayed, I finally came to the conclusion that God's will for Serenity's life was so much better than anything I could even imagine for her. Finally, I prayed the words that had been stuck in my throat for so long "Lord, I do want your will for Serenity's life…even if it means she leaves us."

God certainly didn't need my permission to do anything, but I really believe He just wanted me to trust Him, implicitly trust Him. The next week the whole complexion of the case changed because of an intricate situation that no one knew about. The goal of the case changed from reunification to termination of parental rights. There were still no guarantees that Serenity would be our daughter. The system has rules, ideals, and its own mind. Literally, all we could do was pray, and have every one we knew pray.

There were crazy court dates where people didn't show up and there were legal mistakes that kept the case from moving along, but after a two-and-a-half year roller coaster ride, the termination of parental rights finally happened. It was by all counts an extremely difficult and emotional day. On one hand it was a blessing to know that our daughter would never again have to face the life she had come from, but it was another thing altogether to see a mother lose custody of her children. I know, I know, she had her chance and she blew it time and time again, but for me there was unexplainable heartbreak at the thought that this woman, this mother, would never be a part of her children's lives: never hear them cry or sing a song, never watch them sleep or see them learn something new, never hold them during a storm or kiss a boo-boo. Heartbreaking. Nevertheless, this mom seemed resigned to her fate. She took it in stride. It broke my heart.

There was one final visit between Serenity's mother and her children. It was a day I dreaded. It was a day we prepared Serenity for; Jeff even told her that the "other mother" might be really sad and cry. But that didn't happen. Due to some complicated circumstances, she hadn't seen her children in over a year, and yet it was as if she had seen them the day before. She didn't act or react the way I expected. Then again, I should have known not to "expect" anything. She kissed them, told them she loved them and said goodbye. As I gathered my little group to leave and told everyone to "take a hand," Serenity let go of my hand and grasp the hand of the one who gave her life, sensing that this was an important moment.

At this point in the process, we still had no assurance that we would be able to adopt Serenity. However, a month later we attended a staffing for the case. I don't think I have ever been so nervous or filled with such trepidation. Our caseworker and her supervisor went to bat for us and finally, finally, our hopes and dreams were realized; it was agreed that Serenity would be our daughter forever. Actually, the heavenly Father had been "at bat" for Serenity and for us all along. He wanted us to trust Him! I remembered that, months before, Jeff had prayed that only God would get the glory in this case, no matter what the outcome. That is exactly what happened; He prevailed…no one else could have scripted this story and no one else had a chance. Jeff and I left the DHS office on a cloud with unexplainable joy and such life-giving relief! I told a friend that if we hadn't been in the DHS parking lot with the security guard there, I would have kissed him — (Jeff). She thought I meant kiss the security guard! (I was happy, not crazy!) We called everyone who had been praying through all of our ups and downs for many years. I'm sure the roar could be heard in surrounding states! We were more grateful than we could express and so full of praise.

We thought we could finalize the adoption about three months later and began to plan. However, there were additional problems. Yes, more problems. An appeal and new laws for FBI fingerprint checks made the process go into another year. I felt like I needed to wear a story board explaining our situation! But, what I wrote when THE DAY finally arrived says it all:

February 12, 2008: Well, today was the day! Today was the culmination of three years, four months and six days of waiting, wondering, praying and hoping. Today brought to an end a record-breaking birthing process that was filled with complications. But, as is the case with most birthing experiences, once the child arrives, you forget the complications! Although she was birthed in our hearts a long time ago, today marked the day that Caroline Serenity Erwin was officially "born." Today brought an end to a mountain of frustrations and brought with it a calming voice that whispered to me "no one can ever take her away again!" As our daughter slid under the pews in the courtroom, I stood in awe of a heavenly Father who makes a way for His children, a Father for whom no detail is too small, no dream too big. Today, like the other four days on which my children were born, is a day I will never forget; a day that will define the rest of my life, a day I embrace with joy, peace and intense gratitude for a little girl that entered our lives for a moment, and gets to stay for a lifetime.

Sometimes when I look into my daughter's face, I see myself. She is so much like me. It is what I call a "God thing." Serenity already has such a keen sense of who she is. From about the time she turned two, she realized her skin was different from the rest of us (except Chase after a week at the beach). She began to point out African American people on television or at the store and say, "He's (or she's) black like me." When she was three, she was sitting at the kitchen counter one day while I was cooking. All of a sudden she asked, "Mom, when I grow up, am I going to be white?" I was shaken, but wanted to give an answer that would make sense to a three-year-old. "No, honey," I said. "God made you the way you are with beautiful brown skin. If you were white, you wouldn't be Serenity." That seemed to satisfy her, at least for the time being. A couple of weeks later, she and I were sitting on the sofa talking. For some reason, I decided to tell her that when I was a little girl, I wanted to be a black singer. She looked at me so matter-of-factly and profoundly said "But Mom, then you wouldn't be Christie." Joy filled my heart as I realized that she had not only internalized what I had told her, she understood.

We are blessed beyond measure to call Serenity our daughter. She is a bundle of energy, never meets a stranger, and everyone who knows her loves her. She loves baby dolls and real babies, she absolutely loves to sing and dance, and will do so anytime and anywhere she has a captive audience. After our adoption hearing, we celebrated with a big party at our church for everyone who had been so supportive during the long ordeal. Carson, son of our dear friends, the Harpers, wrote a song for Serenity. It was not just for her, but for all of the children who are in need of a place to call home:

Father

Have you ever been lost?
Have you ever been alone?
Have you been desperate for love?
I have.

Have you ever gone wanting?
Have you ever gone without?
Have you ever felt hopeless and scared?
I have.

Yes I have been waiting
For a home.

But the lost can be found
The lonely need a friend
A mothers best for love
That's what I need.

For gifts at Christmas
For birthdays and cake
For hope and peace
This is what I need.

Yes I have been waiting for a home.

Is there a father for me?
Is there a place I can hide?
Will you open your doors
to this new hopeful life?
I know there'll be trials, but I promise you this
It will be worth it, in the end.

A laugher in the morning
A player in the yard.
A breaker of toys
That's what you need.
A jumper on beds
A smiler at night
A child to call your own
That's what you need.
Yes you have been waiting
For me.

Music and Lyrics 2008 by Carson Richard Harper,
used with permission.

Modern Day Moses

Serenity had been in our home about a month when I got a call about a two-month-old baby boy, the youngest of twelve children. I had said that we would only take one foster child at a time so that we could devote our attention to that child as well as our own biological children. But, there was something different about this call. I just knew deep in my soul that we were supposed to say yes. The investigator that had pulled him from a drug raid was the one who called. I met her on the driveway with a bottle in hand and embraced Kenny for the first time.

Kenny was a joy from the onset. He had the biggest eyes and the most captivating smile. He would melt your heart in a moment. As Serenity ran through the house like a strong wind, Kenny's gentle and easy-going spirit brought wisps of calm. He would press his little head under my neck to go to sleep and loved to just be laid in his bed to rest. And even though we knew he would be reunified with his mother, he was our son. I wanted Kenny's mother to know how much we loved him and that we were praying for her as she diligently and with great intent put her life back together in order to get her children back. She and I forged a relationship that sprang out of two mothers who loved the same little boy. She was so gracious to me as she thanked me for taking care of her son. We couldn't have been more different on the outside, but deep inside both of us loved our children with great passion. I wanted her to know that I didn't judge her; I just wanted to help. She was unbelievable in her pursuit to get her kids back; she kept appointments, didn't miss visitation, got a job, got stable housing, and met all of the court requirements with precision.

One day six months after Kenny came to live with us, the phone rang as Kenny and Serenity both slept in my lap. It was his caseworker calling to tell me that the court had decided he could go home today. "Today?" Although I knew this was a possibility, I didn't internalize it as *the* possibility. I broke down and wept at the thought of never having that little head under my neck again or never being able to look into his crib in the morning to find a bright-eyed, smiley-faced little boy ready for the day. I scrambled to get all of his things together (man, did he have a lot of "things") and began my journey to the DHS office. I made it into the office and unloaded his things, kissed him goodbye and told him how much I loved him. I have to say it was unbearable. My heart was so heavy. I got into my car and began to drive home. Waves of emotion rushed over me as I drove, and I found myself weeping uncontrollably and praying out loud at the same time. I thought about Moses and the short time his mother, Jochebed, was able to care for him. I thought about how hard it must have been for her to let him go to a "Godless" palace, knowing he would not be raised with his family's beliefs and values. I shouted to the Lord, "How could Jochebed have let Moses go?" The Lord answered me so clearly, "Because she knew that the plan I had for Moses was much bigger than hers, and she had faith to trust in Me." That made sense to me and was a great comfort in the months to come.

An incredible thing happened six months after Kenny went back home. I got a call from a caseworker at DHS who told me that Kenny's mother had called earlier that day and asked them to have me call her. This was and is not the norm — this was definitely out-of-the-box. I called her immediately.

"Christie, I wanted you to know that I know how much you guys love Kenny. Any time you would like to pick him up to come and visit you, you can."

Incredible! She didn't have to tell us twice. We took her up on her offer, and a week later we picked up our little "Moses." I wish I could say that it was a phenomenal reunion, but it was very difficult. He wasn't the same smiley-faced little boy with the big afro. He was sullen and tired. After all, he was the youngest of twelve in a household with only one parent. He slept a lot while he was with us. He seemed so sad; he was very cautious and didn't smile at all. Nevertheless, as I sat and rocked him on the first night he was back at our home, I remembered when he left and how much I missed that little soft head under my chin. I reflected on how good God is and how aware He is of not only our needs, but our desires!

Jeff and I agreed that we didn't know if we could continue to have him come. It was just too painful. But our love for Kenny and our desire to be part of his life outweighed our sadness, and we continue to keep him occasionally to this day. It is very hard to think about the struggles in Kenny's life, both for him and for his mother. I want to rescue them both. Truly this is one of the areas in the foster care process where faith comes in, and honestly, faith is critical. I have to repeatedly ask myself, "Do I trust God with this child's life? And do I trust Him enough to leave this child at His feet?" I pray that Kenny will accept Jesus as his Lord and Savior and that he will affect our world in a magnificent way for the Kingdom! I can't wait to see what God is going to do with our "Moses."

Birth Parents

I could not write about my foster care experience without bringing up a group of people, who are often overlooked when talking about foster care: birth mothers. During our eleven years with the agency, all of our babies had birth mothers who had chosen to make an adoption plan. Some of the birth mothers changed their minds, so during the waiting period, the baby was returned to her; nevertheless, it was the birth mother's choice, her decision as to the destiny of her child.

I think often times, even most of the time, that our life experiences dictate our response to our circumstances. Pregnancy is not necessarily a negative to someone who has nothing to call her own. In this day and time, it is much more acceptable, even a right of passage, a status symbol, for an unwed teenage girl to have a baby. But in my experience, it is generally a fantasy that quickly becomes a stark reality once the baby is home and is not just a quiet, cute little doll dressed in Baby Gap clothing. Should every teenager with an unplanned pregnancy choose to place their child for adoption? Of course not. Is choosing to place your child in a home that is ready to parent him/her a sacrificial loving option? Absolutely. How, in the middle of a crisis pregnancy, can Christians reach a young mother with truth, with real options, with love and respect, and with a voice that cries out for the welfare of both the mother and the infant she is carrying? How can we let her know that the heavenly Father knows and cares?

Years ago, I had the opportunity to work with the pregnancy counselor at the agency as she led a study for a group of pregnant young women at a local maternity home. I had always loved, admired, and prayed for the birth mothers of our babies; they were heroes in my eyes, but this was my first experience getting to know birth mothers on a personal level. These young women affected me, heart and soul.

I came home from our first event, outraged and with such righteous indignation. I said to Jeff , "We Christians have no idea what it is like to walk in the shoes of one of these girls!" And we don't. We are critical, judgmental, meddlesome, pharisaical, and just ignorant sometimes when we look at girls with unplanned pregnancies. We know not of what we speak. This hit me that night as I sat in the row of hairdryers as the girls were getting their hair done. One by one they began to share parts of their stories: where they had come from, how they had gotten to this point, and where they wanted to go from here. There was much sadness. There was deep hurt. There was dysfunction. There was fear. And yet, there was hope, as each of them talked about the lives they carried inside of them. I couldn't help but wonder how girls, who in my mind were still children themselves, could mother helpless infants — without support, without guidance, without a shoulder to lean on. Had they made mistakes? Of course. Have I? Definitely. Had they made poor choices? Absolutely. Does that absolve me from any responsibility to minister to them? No. As I got in my car that night, I thought about the church, the body of Christ. Where have we been in the lives of these girls? Why haven't I done more?

Months later, I was with two of these young girls at the hospital as their babies were about to be delivered. I will never forget how utterly alone they both seemed, even in a room full of people. I will never forget standing at the head of the bed when the doctor told the girl to begin pushing; as I stroked her hair gently, she cried, "I can't do this!" I will never forget their little girl faces, as those little girls prepared to become mothers. Little girls placed in women's shoes. I realized that they needed to be mothered, not to become mothers. How I longed to mother them. I know in my life, many times I don't reach out because I don't realize the need. There are also times, quite honestly, when I just don't want to get involved. This experience made me realize how important it is to just "be." We don't have to be experts, we don't have to be professionals, we don't have to be super-moms, we just have to trust our heavenly Father in us and just BE.

I have found that with teenage birth mothers, it is so difficult to judge something for which you have no reference point. It is much easier to make a judgment about the situation than it is to really listen to the heart of the one who is living it. Sometimes you can look deep into the life of a teenage mom and understand why she is the way she is, just by hearing bits and pieces of her story. One such birth mom was a real tough customer — she wasn't going to let people in if it was the last thing she did. She was not my favorite in the program and not one that I had an instant chemistry with, as I did with some of the others. She alienated people: she was arrogant and she was just mean at times. Then, one night, I heard the part of her story that cleared it all up for me. She had lost her mother a couple of years before, a mother she had been extremely close to. As I looked in her eyes and at the newspaper article that talked about her mother's death (an article she had carefully cut out and gently placed in a scrapbook), I got it. She had lost her life, too, when her mother's life was lost. There was no one and nothing that intervened to catch her from the spiral that resulted. I would like to say that things turned around for her, but the last time I heard any word, she had already had two additional pregnancies and was traveling down a road in the wrong direction. My heart still breaks when I think about her.

Many of the girls who are in foster care themselves while they are pregnant and choose to parent their babies, eventually lose their own babies to the system. They have no blueprint for motherhood. Their own mothers have been absent or have failed them in one way or another, or they would not be in foster care. Even a teenage mom with the best intention to raise her child "any way but the way I was raised," will often miss the mark and still follow in the footsteps of her own mother. As I have held such babies in my arms and prayed for those mothers, I have cried out to God about how to break the cycle: of abuse, of self-loathing, of insecurity, of welfare or entitlement, of drug and alcohol addiction, of promiscuity, of worthlessness, of teenage pregnancy. Does this cycle excuse bad decisions or is it a "get out of jail free" card for wrong choices? No. However, it unfortunately results in the birth of precious babies who begin life with baggage that has to be carried by someone. Lord, let me be willing to be that someone.

When we made the change from the agency to the state, the gulf between what my understanding of what a mother should be and the stark reality of what is became wider. These were no longer women who made the choice to place their babies or children for adoption; these were women for whom the choice had been made. We have had children who were rescued from drug raids, dangled over bridges, left at crack houses; who survived abortion attempts, were born in prison, abandoned, or hidden from authorities, who were moved from strange place to strange place and who, more often than not, were born positive for drugs. Most of them have been or will be reunified with the mothers who inflicted these unimaginable horrors on them. Each one of them has made an indelible imprint on my heart and life in a variety of ways, and so have their birth mothers. As I took one of our little ones to the doctor and had seven little vials of blood drawn so that she could be tested for every STD imaginable, I felt my demeanor change. My indignation came to the surface and my intense frustration was all aimed at a birth mom who not only put her own health at risk and contracted an STD, but now had put this frail little one in harm's way as well. I had to reign in my emotions and realize that I had no idea what this woman had been through in her life, what demons she had fought that led her to a life of drug addiction, prostitution and self-destruction — a life that eventually caused her to lose the only thing that she could call her own, her children. Once again, the Lord reminded me that it is not my job to judge; it is my job to be Jesus to those who need Him most. And once again, as I remembered this truth, my heart became more tender toward this birth mother's plight; and regardless of how I felt, the fact was that I was in that place at that time, to love her daughter. Period.

From my perspective, mothers who have had the right to

parent their children stripped away from them because of poor decisions they have made, respond in several ways. They are angry and bitter and indignant. They are depressed and defeated. They feel isolated and small. They can be relieved. I have encountered birth mothers who have personified all of these emotions. One mother was so angry that her children had been taken from her in a drug raid that she wouldn't even tell the investigator what type of formula her baby was taking. But that same birth mother worked diligently on her case plan so that in the shortest amount of time she could get her children back. Slowly, as I took her son, my son, to weekly visits, she and I forged a relationship.

It all began when I included a Christmas gift for her with the diaper bag. It was a very simple gift, a photo album filled with pictures of her son, pictures of the stages in his life she was missing. It was a gift you might expect a foster parent to give a birth parent, an inexpensive gift, a no-fluff gift that seemed so elemental. But it changed the whole complexion of the relationship between the two of us. When I saw her the next time, she wrapped her arms around me and graciously thanked me for the photos; with tears in her eyes she recounted to me how she looked at them every night before she went to sleep. I realized at that moment that I had missed so many opportunities to minister in simple ways that could have made a huge difference. She did get her children back. She and I still see each other occasionally and continue the bond that was created by a little boy with two mothers who love him deeply.

Victim. No other word could describe this birth mother better. She was eleven years old when she became pregnant. Yes, eleven. I found out about her from a friend of a friend who knew I had a heart for young mothers. I had dealt with young mothers before, yes, but this was unconscionable. What I found out next was inexcusable. This child had been exploited by her own birth mother; she had been prostituted for the procurement of drugs. When we met, she had a three-month-old baby: a beautiful, healthy, happy three-month-old baby. My daughter, Cara, (who was about this girl's age at the time) and I, along with two other women, had the great privilege of taking this young mother shopping for clothes. It was a time of sheer joy as we watched her choose clothing, try it on and model it for us. I can still picture her enormous smile as she glided out of the dressing room in each new outfit. Like any pre-teen, she giggled and fidgeted as she and Cara moved in and out of the racks of clothes. Conversely, she was not a typical pre-teen; she was not carefree and responsibility-free; she was a mother. My heart broke as I thought about her life. My heart broke as I thought about her baby's life, a baby that she had decided to "parent." "Parenting" in this case would mean her baby would remain in foster care with her until she turned eighteen. As much as it broke my heart, I could understand why she wanted to keep her baby…her baby was all she had.

This situation would only be a snapshot in my ministry scrapbook, but it would have a lasting impact on my life and the life of my daughter who learned a valuable lesson that day about this world and the people in it, about injustice and the inequity of life.

Vulnerable is not a word I have often used to describe birth mothers who have lost custody of their children to the state. But one teenage mother, who desperately wanted to be seen as "tough" took me by surprise. When I picked up her newborn daughter from the hospital, I learned that she was incarcerated, but I knew little else. I saw her for the first time in court. What

I saw was distressing. She was brought into court in handcuffs and ankle shackles; a necessity to be sure, but heartbreaking. As I sat in the background, holding her baby girl, I tried to put myself in her place. I found it impossible to do. At that moment, she seemed so childlike, so vulnerable, and yet so unredeemable. She had no hope. She did what she had to do to get by, and it was not good. She was raised by an addict mother and had a father in name only. Now, there was a new life brought into this chaotic mess. I had no reference point on which to base an opinion. My heart broke as, once again, I contemplated how in the world I could minister to her; how could I point her to the only One who could redeem her? I have to admit I was fearful of what she would think of me, of my parenting her daughter. I wondered if she would think I was claiming ownership of the one thing in this world that she considered to be hers.

My answer came a few weeks later when she was released and sent to a half-way house for young offenders. The caseworker mentioned in passing that this young mother was very discouraged and that her self-esteem was at an all time low. She was going to be discharged to a foster home herself and had no clothes, no shoes, nothing. That was enough said for me to move my troops into action. My friends, Caryl and Jan, and I hit the stores. We split up and each found an outfit; Jan, of course, had to accessorize hers to the hilt, complete with purse and earrings. I also purchased a Bible and had her name embossed on it. It seemed like the right thing to do. I loaded it all up and dropped it off for the caseworker to take to her. Later that night, my cell phone rang with a number I did not recognize. It was the half-way house. They asked if it would be okay for this young woman to speak to me. Taking the phone, she spoke softly as she told me how much she appreciated the clothing and how much it meant to her. I was overwhelmed by the impact this simple gesture had on her life. As with so many of these girls, she needed a mother. As I talked to her, I understood how alone she was in this world, an aloneness that caused her to search in all the wrong places for validation, fulfillment, hope, and most of all, love.

I would like to say this situation had a fairy tale ending, but it didn't. She did get her daughter back, for a time. She parented her the way she was 'parented,' and it was horrible. It was so hard for me to hear about my little "daughter" going through the things she was going through and I was impotent to do anything about it. This mother's life spiraled downward into the same lifestyle that had begun this havoc. We got the baby back for a second time. The good news is that a family member took guardianship of "our" baby. The bad news is this young mother's search for significance, for freedom and for salvation continues.

An interesting phenomenon that has held me captive throughout our journey in foster care is fathers, or the lack there-of. I have to admit that there is immense frustration as I think of what birth mothers have to bear versus what birth fathers "bear." How can we as Christians challenge men to step up to the plate in the lives of their children? How can we impress upon them what a critical role fathers play in the lives of their children and what a lasting impact a father's love (or lack thereof) has on a child? I have come out of court with such outrage after hearing testimony from a birth father who testified that he "no longer had any relationship with the birth mother of his son." He just stopped by the house every once in a while to "give her a little money, a little somethin', somethin'"… only to find out later that the little somethin', somethin' was another son, baby number ten to a woman who had already lost several to the system.

It makes me want to scream.

All of the men in my life have been men of integrity. And I know how blessed I am. These men would give everything to meet the needs of their families; men who live life with loyalty and fidelity and selflessness, as their mantras. Are they perfect men? Heavens, no. But they are men who take responsibility for the lives God has entrusted to them. And I trust them. Because this is my experience, I have little understanding and little patience for a man who is nothing more than a sperm donor in the life of a child. I know that sounds harsh, but my experience with the foster care system has characterized these men as indifferent, unavailable, disinterested, proud, and selfish! Not one of our babies has had a father in the home. Not one of them has had a father who was married to the mother. Not one of them has had a father who was interested in being a part of that child's life. Not one.

I am guessing that most of the eyes that are reading these words are the eyes of women: (and that is great!); however, I don't want to let this part of the book go by without challenging you. Let me say right now that if you are a married foster mother, give your husband a hug and let him know how important he is in the life of each child who comes through your door. Granted, we as mothers may give most of the day-to-day care of the children placed in our home, but don't underestimate the influence your husband has. He is an integral piece to the puzzle of this child's life, a piece; that may never be replaced once the child has gone. He may be the ONLY father that child ever knows, the only "book" they ever read on fatherhood. Your husband, my husband, may be the only example of an earthly father who can point that child to the heavenly Father. Talk about an important job. It is critical.

I know in our ministry, especially at the beginning, it seemed to be my ministry, my calling and honestly it was. Jeff was so willing to get behind me and allow me to pursue what God was telling me to do. And quite frankly, there have been times when he has had to hold me up and to carry me. Times of grief, of anger, of frustration; times when I had no sleep and no hope of any; times when no one seemed to understand my persistent passion. He was and is my rock. But as a couple there are also the rough times. Times when we have no time together, when the sound of a baby's cry is much more common than the sound of a love song. There are times when the system stalls, and the spirit in our home seems to wane, when selfishness and self-pity overshadow what God has ordained. These times are the times Satan loves. The enemy loves to take good and turn it to evil. He wants to see us agitated, grumpy, self-indulgent and too tired to do our Master's will. Boy, have I experienced those times. It is in those times when the Father quietly says (or sometimes He has to shout over the noise), "Christie, remember the call; this is not about you."

But over the years I have seen my ministry turn into our ministry. I have watched my precious husband in the early years, rush to the car to throw the empty car-seat in the trunk, because he knew what a painful reminder it was to me. I have watched him rest babies in the special little groove in his arm and rock them for hours on end. I have heard him pray for and bless each child that has been in our home, and I have seen the father of my children be a real father, for whatever length of time, to over forty other children. What an incredible blessing as a wife to see God work through the man you love! When we made the move to the state, in the front of his Bible, Jeff began keeping a picture of each of the babies who left our home. Although he is no longer their father, he knows Who is and lifts them up often to the One who made them; trusting Him to protect them, to provide for them, and to one day draw them to Himself. Think I'll go give Jeff a hug.

Convictions and Confessions

CHAPTER THIRTEEN

*A*fter fifteen years what do I know about foster children? I know that they have entered this foster care journey through no fault of their own, and they don't deserve to be stigmatized for the indiscretions and inadequacies of their parents. They are special. They are unique. They are each one-of-a-kind with special talents, gifts and potential. All of those things may be untapped and underdeveloped, but they are there nonetheless.

They deserve a voice. Not a quiet, meek, timid, and reserved voice, but a resounding and reverberating cry for justice, for unconditional love and the right to live in safety and peace. Granted, that voice may not be their own, but they deserve to have someone embrace their cause and make sure it is heard. They deserve to be valued, to know that value and have it instilled in them. They deserve to internalize the truth that they are worth fighting for.

Foster children deserve to be known in a deep, non-condemning, unconditional-loving way. Their feelings deserve validation — all feelings, no matter how trivial or how horrific they may be. They deserve to be number one in someone's life. They deserve to be loved with everything I have as a parent: the sold out, no-holds-barred love, without the presumption of receiving something in return, without condition, regardless of their behavior, attitude or actions.

Foster children deserve to be protected. They deserve the right to be children, not little adults who have to shoulder the responsibilities of a household or of younger siblings, of teenage pregnancy, of the moral indiscretions of others, of parents who are more like children than they are. Foster children need to be hugged, kissed, nurtured, taught, played with, sung to, tucked in at night, and brought before the Father. And they deserve that.

Sometimes it is hard for me to understand how the view of foster children in our society has become so skewed. We have devalued these children based on our own preconceived ideas about who and what they are. They are a product of their environment. It is not fair to penalize them for things over which they have had no control. It is not fair to judge them on our personal scale as to what a child should or should not be or do. This judgment is the result of seeing foster children through human eyes and not the eyes of the Father. Perhaps if I weren't so intimately involved in this issue, I could understand it more, or at least stomach it. Most people have no idea what foster children have gone through, and personally I don't think most of us want to know. It's just too painful.

This concept was never more real to me than the time I

was co-chairing an event in our county to showcase the need for adoptive families. It was a "Heart Gallery" event where pictures, beautiful professionally done pictures, of the children who were awaiting adoption in our county were displayed. I volunteered to prepare brief adoption summaries to accompany the pictures. As I waded through tons of paperwork, my heart broke as I read page after page of unspeakable things that had happened to bring children into care. My mind tried to take these things in, but my heart wouldn't let it. I just could not picture innocent children suffering at the hands of the very people that were supposed to love and protect and cherish them. These were not unintentional acts but deliberate, heinous violations that made me cringe: broken bones, incest, filth, solicitation. And although these children are not responsible for what happened to them in their past, they are left with only remnants with which to create a future. Those remnants may be fear, Reactive Attachment Disorder, Attention Deficit Hyperactivity Disorder, Oppositional Defiant Disorder, sexually transmitted diseases, self-loathing, guilt, teenage pregnancy, mental illness, drug addiction, lack of education, depression, hopelessness — the list is endless. On the other hand, foster children are just like any other children. They want to have fun, to grow up healthy and strong with enough food to eat and the proper clothes to wear. They want to enjoy life, to have friends and to have a family that loves and protects them. You need look no farther than their eyes to see the longing in their hearts for permanence, for a "place."

The distorted view of foster children is not limited to the general public! A friend of mine had her two-year-old foster son with her one day at church. A lady asked about him and made the comment that in our little circle still lives in infamy; "Oh, he's too cute to be a foster child!" What? On another day, I was out shopping with my four-month-old foster son, when a clerk at the store began to ask questions about him. She then made a comment that made the hairs on my neck stand up, "But, he's so clean and everything!"

Judging from just these two comments, all foster children should be ugly and dirty. Righteous indignation rules in my being when comments like this are made. In fact, maybe it's not "righteous" at all! At times like these, my usually calm, peace-making, non-confrontational manner morphs into that of a mama bear whose cubs are threatened. I just want to stand up and scream, "These children are gifts; they are children of God who are precious in His sight, and in mine; they are special and are not second best to anyone!" Oh Lord, that we would all understand the enormous value of each of these little lambs and never, ever, take for granted how much you love them and how important they are to you.

"Oh Lord, Thou hast searched me and known me.
Thou dost know when I sit down and when I rise up;
Thou dost understand my thought from afar.
Thou dost scrutinize my path and my lying down,
And art intimately acquainted with all my ways.
Even before there is a word on my tongue,
Behold, O Lord, Thou does know it all.
Thou hast enclosed me behind and before,
And laid Thy hand upon me.
Such knowledge is too wonderful for me;
It is too high, I cannot attain it."
Psalm 139:1-6

"For Thou didst form my inward parts;
Thou didst weave me in my mother's womb.
I will give thanks to Thee,
for I am fearfully and wonderfully made;
Wonderful are Thy works,
And my soul knows it very well.
My frame was not hidden from Thee,
When I was made in secret,
And skillfully wrought in the depths of the earth.
Thine eyes have seen my unformed substance;
And in Thy book they were written,
The days that were ordained for me,
When as yet there was not one of them."
Psalm 139:13-16

There are times, however, if I am honest, when everything that I believe foster children are and everything I believe foster children deserve is tested to the very core of my soul. The enemy knows my weakness. When I am tired, when I am stressed, when I have picked up the same book ten times in one afternoon, or have been slapped in the face by a one-year-old; when my toddler puts his toothbrush in the toilet and then his mouth, when I've had no time with the Father: when I've slept too little, eaten too much and exercised…well, none — those are the times that I am faced with my selfishness. And I have to reach deep inside and cry out to the Lord to renew me, to carry me, to refresh my call and energize my commitment to do what He has called me to do. Quite frankly, it isn't easy. I am so blessed to have my sisters in ministry, Caryl, Donna, and Jan who have seen me cry more than any other people, (except my precious husband and incredible parents). They know what to say and what to do when they answer the phone and hear nothing but my sobs on the other end. We carry each other. We carry each other through the joys, the craziness, and the profound sorrow that is foster care. No one understands like they do because they have lived it. They know me, as well. They know I don't like confrontation. They know I take on more than I can handle sometimes, and often, it's not pretty! They know I love to shop and that baby clothes are my favorite. They know I am passionate about my family, about my ministry, and about foster children specifically. They know that as a child I wanted to be a black singer when I grew up, and they are still holding out hope with me! Together they form a lifeboat that has carried me safely home many times. I love them dearly and am so grateful that we are sharing this journey together.

In my life, being a foster parent has been an incredible gift. As my friend Donna says, it is what I was "born to do"! It is unbelievable to think that the Lord would choose to use me, someone who is so fallible, inadequate, and unworthy, to care for these children that He holds so dear. I remember reading somewhere that often times God does His greatest work through frail people. That is how I feel. It is nothing short of amazing! I am blessed beyond measure.

After fifteen years, what have I learned about myself and the call on my life to be a foster parent? I have been overwhelmed with love, joy and excitement, and been flung down with grief. I have been amazed at the support of those around me and been astounded at the prejudice that still exists in our world today. I have watched as my children nurture, comfort, fall in love with, and pray for each little child that is ours for a time. I have realized my weakness and the Lord's magnificent strength. I have come to understand that, as in all ministry opportunities, there are many sacrifices involved in the foster care process. These sacrifices come in various forms. There is lack of sleep, lack of quality family time, lack of intimate time with my husband, lack of time for myself. There are times when we can't attend functions with our friends, because we have little ones, and well, at our age, nobody else does. There is fear, frustration and the feeling at times that no one understands.

And finally, there is the unexplainable grief, the deep feeling of loss, the death of a relationship and the worries that accompany the grief. Will this child wonder where I am and why I've left him? Will this child be safe physically, emotionally, spiritually? Will this child have enough food to eat and the proper clothes to wear? Will this child be loved and protected? Will this child ever have the opportunity to achieve his/her God-given potential? Will this child know that God loves him/her and will he/she ever come to know Jesus? Will this child ever know how much I love him/her? In the midst of all of these unanswered questions comes the penetrating truth that God is in control. He is able. He has a plan. And He is sufficient. He always sends people and circumstances to encourage and sustain me in times of despair.

Then there is the frustration of dealing with the "system." It may surprise you, but our governmental system is flawed! I referred to our foster care experience with the agency as the "country club of foster care." When we made the move to the state, we lost our "country club membership."

There is injustice, lack of concern for our feelings, and a sense at times that no one understands or even cares. The caseworkers are overworked, overloaded, underpaid and underappreciated. There is not enough money in the world to pay these people to see and do what they have to see and do on a daily basis. We have encountered workers who are self-less, brave, loving, and passionate about the work they do and about their "kids." We have loved them, they have loved us, and we still call them friends. But we have also known workers who were power-hungry, prejudiced, and who would take personal offense at any suggestion that we — as the 24/7 caregivers — thought was best for the child. Once again, if we get down to basics, it's not about us; it's about the kids! Navigating the system seems much less daunting when the life of a child is at stake, and I find myself much more outspoken when the rights of a child have been overlooked or even violated. I feel strongly that as believers it is not necessarily our job to try to change the system. It is our job to serve the children and the workers within that system, to make a difference in their lives because Jesus has made a difference in our lives. I guess what I am saying is that a broken system is no reason, no excuse, to neglect intervening on a child's behalf; it only makes God's provision for that child so much sweeter.

One thing I know about foster care and adoption is that the blessings far outweigh the sacrifice. I am only doing what God has called me to do; He's doing the rest. I decided years ago to throw myself, my whole self, into the call that God placed on my heart. However, in doing this, every time I embrace a child, I choose to make myself vulnerable; vulnerable enough to make mistakes, to fail, to doubt, to fear, and at times to lose hope, but ultimately to trust the heavenly Father to work in this unequipped, disorganized, humorous housewife! I have felt God's power in my life in a tangible way as I have wrapped my arms around each baby and I have felt His arms wrap around me as I let them go. In my life, foster care has been an extraordinary testimony to the heavenly Father, a testimony to His faithfulness,

His omnipotence, His power, His mercy and to the intricacies of His plan for our lives.

I know that fostering for the state is exactly where I, where we as a family, are supposed to be. There is absolutely NO question about that. I know that God chose to move our family's ministry to the state for a purpose, and I know beyond a shadow of a doubt that Serenity is the cornerstone of that purpose.

The "call" and The C.A.L.L., and The Christmas C.A.L.L.

CHAPTER FOURTEEN

About two years into our ministry with the state, I was invited to a summit meeting at an area church. The purpose of the summit was to discuss the possibility of combining efforts by churches in our county to help in some way with our state's foster care system. Incredibly, this summit would lead to a new unprecedented initiative that would eventually be known as The C.A.L.L. (Children of Arkansas Loved for a Lifetime) www.the-callinarkansas.org. With great enthusiasm, I attended the meeting, and Jeff and I got involved in The C.A.L.L. from the very beginning. The premise was that The C.A.L.L. would be a co-operative effort between local churches and the Department of Children and Family Services. Our job at the church level would be to recruit foster and adoptive families, guide them through the process, train them, support them, and encourage them. DCFS would allow us to train our own "trainers" for the foster/adoptive parent classes and allow us to hold those training sessions on our timetable within a church setting while giving us the support we needed to do those things.

As we began sorting out our goals, our expectations, and our hopes and dreams for The C.A.L.L., we saw God's hand in everything we did. He put into place a new DCFS director that embraced this concept whole heartedly and passionately. He brought together a group of DCFS attorneys, caseworkers, supervisors, and administrators who had open minds and open hearts to any group of people who wanted to aid them in meeting the needs of the children in their care. They were not only willing to think outside the box, but they were willing to get their hands dirty in the process. He called believers from many different denominations to be church representatives for The C.A.L.L. at their local church, all led by the executive director, Mary Carol Pedersen, a passionate former foster parent. He began weaving all of us together — each of us individual threads from different spools — into a one-of-a-kind tapestry! We all "put our hands to the good work."

When we began the process of informing and educating evangelical churches in our county about the efforts of The C.A.L.L., we determined that our God-sized goal would be that within two years from the inception of The C.A.L.L., there would be no waiting children in our county. That is, no children who were waiting on an appropriate foster care placement, and no children waiting to be adopted. As people began to hear about The C.A.L.L. and, more importantly by the need for foster and adoptive families in our city, county, and state, they were surprised at the great need; they were overwhelmed by the number of children in foster care; and most of all, they were convicted. We heard story after story from people who had had no prior thoughts of fostering or adopting, but when the plea was given, the Holy Spirit tugged at their heartstrings and made it clear about what they were supposed to do. There were other people who had been thinking about fostering or adopting for years and just needed a little nudge to step up to the line and make the commitment. Although the target date for our goal is not here yet, The C.A.L.L. is well on its way to making a profound and lasting difference in the lives of the children in our state. On a personal note, remember "The Alex Project"? God continues to allow me to see the different pieces of the puzzle of my ministry gently being put together by His hand, in His time, in the order in which He chooses, and being molded into the configuration He desires. To God be the glory!

Shortly after The C.A.L.L. began (two months in fact) the staff at DHS informed us of the great need for Christmas presents for foster children. It was something I had never really thought much about. Jeff and I had always treated our foster children as our own and bought Christmas gifts for them on the same (sometimes excessive!) level as our own children. But apparently that was not the case in many situations. We were told that many times caseworkers would be scrambling around on Christmas Eve trying to gather up gifts for the children in their caseloads.

"That is ridiculous," I thought to myself, "There are too many people that I know who would be willing and excited to give so that foster children have a special Christmas!"

One of the ladies involved in The C.A.L.L. took it upon herself to organize the effort that first year. I was excited to assist her with the overall process and be in charge of the "push" at our church. Here are two of the many unbelievable experiences that I had the first year of "The Christmas C.A.L.L.":

It was Christmas 2006. The C.A.L.L. was in infancy, but was made aware of the incredible need for Christmas gifts for foster children. We threw together a plan and began to ask church members to meet the needs of these kids. At our church, we set up a little Christmas tree with ornaments that had the child's name, age and wish list. The outpouring of love was unbelievable! One couple really touched my heart as I 'manned' the little tree. They were newlyweds, married a little over a year and both students. They casually took two of the ornaments with a smile. Later in the week, the wife called and said, "Do you have any more ornaments? We had so much fun buying for our two. We've bought Christmas gifts for our families and we have some money left. We don't need anything, so we'd like another name." I explained that the only lists left were teenagers with expensive items, but told her she could take a look.

As the deadline for turning in gifts drew near, she and her husband came by our house. When I opened the door, there they stood as if they had won the lottery. They came in with sacks in hand and a beautiful bicycle that wasn't the run-of-the-mill $29.95 special, but a cool green dirt bike perfect for a boy who was probably used to run-of-the-mill. And then it came...they handed me a small sack. I will never

*forget their eyes, their glowing faces, their uncon-
ditional love for a teenager they will never meet. I
opened the sack. An iPod. An iPod for an 18-year-
old boy who, in the world's mind was ready to age
out of the system. An I-POD that was more than just
a gift; it was an expression of hope, of purpose, of
love and the willing sacrifice of a young couple who
reached beyond their own needs to fulfill the desire
of one eighteen- year-old who expected his list to
go unfilled.*

*Abby and Ethan were one and two years old
when their parents took the names of two foster children off of our little tree. Little did their parents know
that not only would the lives of the two foster children be affected by their actions, but their own children's lives would be changed as well. Who would
have thought that a one-year-old and a two-year-old
could understand the needs of two little children who
had been thrust into the unknown world of foster
care? Who could have known that a one-year-old
and a two-year-old would take into their tiny hearts
the angst of two other tiny hearts as they prayed for
them in simple childlike faith, night after night, long
after Christmas had passed? Who could have seen
the difference that those gifts made in the lives of
ones who had so little, and who could see the difference those prayers would make on souls who had
lost so much? The answer is simple… He saw and He
sees. The One for whom all gifts are ultimately given,*

> *the One who is "the Gift" takes what little we have*
> *to offer Him and multiplies it beyond our wildest*
> *expectation. He knows what difference Abby and*
> *Ethan's persistent prayers will make in the lives of*
> *two children they will probably never meet. And on*
> *the other side of eternity, Abby and Ethan will*
> *know too.*

The next year, it was my turn to steer the ship! My friend, Jan, and I took on the huge responsibility of making sure the foster children in our county had a Christmas they would never forget.

This responsibility came at an interesting time in the life of our family. Not only did we have Serenity's adoption pending, but we had an eighteen-month-old foster son and a four-month-old foster daughter. (We had never had so many children in our home before, but for reasons I can't really explain, it was what God had ordained for that time!)

As Jan and I began laying out the plan for year two of The Christmas C.A.L.L., we began seeing God's provision everywhere we turned. We saw Him move in the lives of churches; we saw Him touch individuals as He turned selfishness into selflessness, and we saw Him wrap His arms around the people at DHS who are so often overlooked.

It was a crazy and intense time. My entire house was filled with Christmas gifts. At one time there were twenty-one bicycles in my living room and dining room. I felt like I lived and worked at the North Pole! There were Game Boys, X-boxes, PlayStations, iPods, stereos, dolls, clothes, games, books, bicycles, tricycles, jewelry, skates, coats, and a million other gifts! In the end, C.A.L.L. churches filled the Christmas lists of over seven hundred children in our county! Two caseworkers made these comments:

> *"I want to express my deepest gratitude to the families that donated all the wonderful and generous gifts to all the foster children on my caseload. These children were so happy and the older children were at a loss for words. There have been gifts donated before, but nothing ever like this to my children. These children got better gifts than I did. (Smile.) But, again I want to thank you all for your kindness and sincerity, because you all did not have to, but I am glad you did. I hope to work with all the beautiful families again this year. Bless you all."*

> *"I had the opportunity to share in the gifts of love we received with one of my special needs children that your organization sponsored. My heart was overwhelmed at how she had such patience in opening her gifts, trying not to tear the paper. She was so excited when she finally got them opened to see her dolls and the accessories. She really loved the books! God bless you all for your generosity and expressions of love to our foster children."*

Perhaps one of the most rewarding by-products of The Christmas C.A.L.L. was the impact it had on the caseworkers themselves. We had determined that not only did the foster children need to feel loved and appreciated during the Christmas season, but so did the DHS staff. Each church that took a list of children also took the names of the caseworker(s) responsible for those children. We gave caseworkers and other DHS staff gift cards, notes, and other tokens of encouragement and appreciation. After Christmas, a caseworker wrote to me about her experience. Her words punctuated my comments about the importance of not only living out the life of Christ for foster children, but for those caseworkers and administrators that are in the trenches every day and never hear a word of affirmation.

"One of my foster children had a really great Christmas this year. You guys were the icing on the cake for a 13-year-old girl on my case load. This girl got to go back home just a few days before Christmas! She was SO happy! She had the gifts from The C.A.L.L. waiting on her at the office to take home with her as well. The day the judge ordered that she go back with her family, she had to go back to the office to pick up those gifts so that she could celebrate when she got home that night and got to sleep in her own bed. It was a great day and to have Christmas gifts made it even greater!

And on a personal note from me... this Christmas season was very stressful for me. When I got back from transporting a child, I walked back into the office and opened the $50 gift card to Wal-Mart! What? That was a surprise! I had NO money for gifts for my very supportive family this year. So, I went to Wal-Mart and bought little things for all of my family members with that gift card. It just really *meant a lot to me during a very stressful time. Thanks to all of the people and churches involved in providing gifts for the deserving foster kids in our county and for making my life better during Christmas, too!"*

Although it was an exhausting time, I felt that I had experienced the truth of the Christmas season. My heart was so full it overflowed. The outpouring of love and sacrificial giving was a testimony to the hearts of God's people: a need was presented and God's people willingly and enthusiastically responded.

The Adoption Coalition and The Heart Gallery

A month before Serenity's adoption was finalized, the adoption supervisor in our county asked me if I would attend a meeting of our county's adoption coalition. The coalition was created to be a conduit for adoption in our county. It is made up of DHS workers, attorneys, child welfare professionals, foster parents, adoptive parents and anyone interested in facilitating adoptions for the children in our county. Although I didn't know at the time exactly what the coalition was or did, I graciously accepted the offer to attend; after all, I was about to be an adoptive parent! I took our five-month-old foster daughter with me and sat down to observe the goings-on. Little did I know that this supervisor had a diabolical plan (only joking)...she was going to nominate me to co-chair the coalition! I heard my name, but thought, "Surely, she didn't just say 'Christie Erwin.'" But she had. As strange as it sounded, I heard myself accept the nomination for a position that I knew nothing about, on a coalition that I knew nothing about! Nevertheless, from the moment I accepted, I knew that was where I was supposed to be and that the coalition was the next stop on my ministry road trip.

I felt my passion rise as I contemplated getting to be a part of finding homes for the children in our county that needed them. My mind began to race as I thought about ways we could get the word out, and my heart was full of excitement, even if I was clueless about what to do next.

As I began to learn more about the organization I was helping to head-up, I found out that the coalition had begun a Heart Gallery for our county. Heart Galleries have been popping up all over the United States. A Heart Gallery is a presentation of professional photographs of children whose parental rights have been terminated and who are ready and waiting for an adoptive family. In our county the photographs are displayed individually (Some are of sibling groups.) on easels with information about the child. A Heart Gallery can be incredibly effective, deeply heart wrenching and intensely soul stirring, as people come face to face with "real live" children in need of permanent loving homes.

I was captivated by the concept. I knew that it was important for people to see the faces of the children in our county who needed permanence, a place to call home. So, my first order of business as co-chairman of the adoption coalition was to plan, prepare, and execute the official Pulaski County Adoption Coalition 2008 Heart Gallery Premiere.

The premiere was an unforgettable night. It was a night of passion and compassion. It was a night where the real heart of the children's judicial system in our county was seen. It was a night when ordinary people embraced the cause and eventually became extraordinary parents to extraordinary children whose pictures captured their hearts. I was blessed beyond measure to be a part of such an incredible night.

What happened next was nothing short of a miracle! We asked the churches that were involved in The C.A.L.L. if they would like to host the gallery in their individual churches. From February until June, we did not have one available date left on our "Heart Gallery Tour Date Calendar!" Caryl, my dad and I moved (and continue to move) the easels (lovingly known as 'pick-up-sticks' for the way they seem to always intertwine in transit) and the photographs from church to church to church. It has been a labor of love to be sure, but it has become a very personal project for all of us. Each week as we move our kids' pictures we pray. We pray for them for each one to be given a family, a place…a home. We sometimes asked each other why. Why has no one inquired about Johnny or Susie? We ache when we see that most of the time, when we return to move the gallery to another location, the information sheets on younger children are gone, but the information sheets on the teenagers are hardly touched. Then we are reminded that we are entrusted with the great honor of making sure the faces of our kids are seen.

Not only are we entrusted with this honor, but Jan, Donna, Caryl and I have had the opportunity to transport children to the Heart Gallery photo shoots as well. For all of us these have been heart-wrenching and emotional times that have cemented our commitment to the foundation of finding families for these kids. They have also been touching times for us as we get to meet some of the children whose photographs we will be moving week to week, praying for, and "Lord willing" finding a forever family for. The first two times I drove children to the photo shoot, both of them wanted to be adopted by me. I was beginning to get a big head until it dawned on me that I was the one taking them out for lunch and letting them order whatever they wanted. I realized that it wasn't so much about me after all, it was about the food I had to offer!

A few months ago, I drove a twelve-year-old African American boy whom I'll call Mike, to have his picture taken for The Heart Gallery. He was a strong, robust boy, yet so gentle and mannerly. He understood his situation well: his parental rights had been terminated and he was available for adoption. We stopped by to get some lunch on the way back to his school and had a great conversation. I wasn't ready for the poignant question he asked as I was about to drop him off, "How long will it be before I get adopted?" My heart broke as I thought about all he had been through and the uncertainty that must follow him wherever he goes. As I thought about that tough question, deep inside my spirit cried, "No child should ever have to ask that question." I pray that Mike will never have to ask it again! My prayer is that God will swoop down, rescue him and cause his life to be completely changed because of a family chosen just for him.

Last week we had another photo shoot. It was an incredible morning filled with twenty-two beautiful, rowdy kids being corralled to have their pictures taken. My SUV was filled with a sibling group of four; Donna went to two locations to pick up two toddlers, and Caryl made her way out to the country to pick up a teenage girl that I'll call Angela. After needing a GPS system and making several phone calls to get to where she was going, Caryl finally made it to our destination. Angela was so pretty and well-mannered. She held my foster daughter and talked about how gorgeous she was, and then she had her picture taken and left.

A few minutes later, Caryl called me in tears, "Christie, what are we going to do? How else are we going to get the word out about the need for adoptive families? This just breaks my heart!"

She went on to relay a conversation she had with Angela. They had stopped to buy lunch as Caryl returned Angela to her foster home. Caryl's adopted daughter, Mariah, was with her and Angela was intrigued by the relationship between Mariah and Caryl's biological children.

Angela asked Caryl, "Is Mariah spoiled?"

"Yes, she is, in fact. Everybody should get the chance to be spoiled!" Caryl answered.

"I never have," Angela replied with tears running down her face.

"Well, I'm going to spoil you today," Caryl responded. "You can order anything on the menu! And, Angela, I want you to know that it's not your fault, nothing you did brought you into foster care. I also want you to know that I will be praying for you."

As Caryl expressed her concern for Angela and her frustration at the fact that there are so many teenagers in our county that need families, a sense of renewed commitment came over me. "We have got to find families for these children," I thought, "their very lives and futures depend on it."

That is what the Heart Gallery is all about. It is such a simple concept: find families for available children. That is my heart, my passion. As you read these words, please pray for the children whose pictures I am moving every week (Visit us at www.pulaskicountyadoptioncoalition.com.) Pray for the children whose pictures are in a gallery in your area. And while you are at it, ask the Lord if you are the answer to one of these prayers!

"Lord, may all of our Heart Gallery frames be empty."

The Challenge

CHAPTER SIXTEEN

If you haven't realized it by now, all of our children have first names that begin with "C" (Chase, Caleb, Cara, Connor, Caroline Serenity), so I decided to try to condense my thoughts down to my ten C's for foster care and/or adoption. Each of these "C" words has special meaning in my life and ministry, and I pray that they will ring true in your life as well.

The first "C" is for Calling. Once you become a Christian, having accepted Jesus Christ as your personal Lord and Savior, you are given spiritual gifts. Along with these gifts, I feel that we all have a mission, a ministry, for which we have been set aside. For some it is in the work place, for others it is on the mission field or the classroom; for many it is within the walls of the church building, but for others it has a broader scope in the community. If you are one of these "community" folks, I would challenge you to look into foster care and/or adoption in your city and state. Conversely, do not feel pressured to minister in this way. If you have been called to foster or adopt, you will know it. I don't want to be an alarmist, but I have met many people who enter into fostering with great and noble intentions, only to quit when a child or the system is not what they expected. Foster care and adoption are great concepts, but they are not just great concepts. It sounds so awesome to get to be a part of helping a child in need, and it is an unexplainable blessing, but the concept sometimes falters when the reality sets in and a child comes into your care. This is the time to remember once again that it is not about you (or me). It is my prayer that your heart has been pricked by my experience and that you would begin to pray about what effect you and your family can have in the life of a child that needs you. No one may understand the call on your life, other than you and the Father! Trust the Lord inside of you and do what He says to do.

The second "C" is Confirmation. God will confirm what He wants for your life. In my life, he confirmed the ministry with a series of events, through His Word, and by the wise guidance of the people who knew me best. All of these things pointed me in the direction I knew God wanted me to go.

On to the third "C"— Commitment. God asked me to commit before I even knew what I was committing to. It was an act of faith to be sure, but it was mostly an act of obedience. After a few years of fostering, however, I had this overwhelming sense of being all alone in this. I felt that no one really understood why in the world I would want to put myself through this process and loss again and again; why, when I already had four biological children would I want to take on another one, one who wasn't even mine. As I sat in church one morning with these self-serving thoughts running through my head, the Lord spoke clearly to me, "You do have people who understand and who care, but even if you didn't, it's what I have called you to do, and you must do it." With those words, a sense of resignation came over me. I would look to that morning many times in the years to come as I planted my feet firmly on the ground of the commitment to what God had called me to do. It has also been important for me to continue to revisit the commitment, to renew the commitment and rededicate myself to the commitment. The commitment I made fifteen years ago doesn't look much like the one I am living today; it has evolved and has been honed over time. The commitment has been met at times with closed doors, but as those doors have closed, others have swung wide open.

One of my favorite "C's" is Comfort Zone. How many times do we get to do something important for the Father without getting out of our comfort zone? Not many I would say! I have found myself outside of mine many times. I think the Lord uses removing us from our comfort zone to test our faith, our stamina, and our commitment to whatever cause He has asked us to take up. It is exhilarating to step out of ourselves and let the Father exert control. There is a strong feeling of satisfaction and triumph in letting God move us as we simply rest in Him.

Compassion is critical in the Christian life. It is critical in meeting the needs of children and their birth families as well. People in this world want authenticity. They want to know that "what they see is what they get." People know when you have compassion for them versus when you are passing judgment. God has been so gracious to me, and I want to pass that on to others. Do I always succeed? I think you can find a resounding "NO" to that question in the pages of this book! But it is my desire to live life with the hands, feet and touch of my Savior. Isaiah 58 has been an integral Scripture in my thinking regarding compassion (and it even comes with promises):

"Is this not the fast which I chose,
To loosen the bonds of wickedness,
To undo the bands of the yoke,
And to let the oppressed go free,
And break every yoke?
Is it not to divide your bread with the hungry,
And bring the homeless poor into the house;
When you see the naked, to cover him;
And not hide yourself from your own flesh?
Then your light will break out like the dawn,
And your recovery will speedily spring forth;
And your righteousness will go before you;
The glory of the Lord will be your rear guard.
Then you will call, and the Lord will answer;
You will cry, and He will say 'Here I am.'"
Isaiah 58:6-9

"And if you give yourself to the hungry,
And satisfy the desire of the afflicted,
Then your light will rise in darkness,
And your gloom will become like midday.
And the Lord will continually guide you,
And satisfy your desire in scorched places,
And give strength to your bones;
And you will be like a watered garden,
And like a spring of water whose waters do not fail."
Isaiah 58:10-11

The word Convenience is something we in America know a lot about. We like things in our lives to be convenient; in fact, we expect it. We balk when there is too much work involved! We want to sit back, enjoy ourselves and let the dishes wash, the clothes dry, the instant potatoes mash, the garage door open, and the remote control change the channel. However, ministry opportunities in my life seem to come at some of the most inconvenient times! I have learned through the years that these times are only inconvenient to me and that God's plans are always right on time. And like me, I've heard people use every excuse in the book to keep from ministering through foster care. "I'm going to wait until my youngest child starts to school, or my oldest child goes to college, or until I finish this or that, or have a little more money." If you wait for those things to happen, you will never jump in; something else will take the place of those excuses. And they are excuses. My advice to you is if you are called to foster or adopt, do it. It's as simple as that. Either you obey or you don't. I'm sure that the apostle Peter didn't think it was convenient to drop the net full of fish that he had worked so hard to catch in order to follow Jesus! But, like Peter, we've got to be willing to drop everything and follow His plan. What is keeping you from following? What is your "net?" Second Timothy 4:2 says to be ready "in season and out of season, when it is convenient and when it is not." (The Way, The Living Bible)

Confrontation is the next "C." Often following God's call causes us to have to confront. Confrontation is not something I welcome. It has never expressed who I am, even if it is sometimes necessary, and I hate it. But I have found that the more my passion for foster children sizzles, the easier it is for me to confront on their behalf. There are times when I can feel the passion rising. As a foster parent or adoptive parent, what might you have to confront? There are a host of things: the world's view of children in foster care, the view of children in foster care by the body of Christ, family members that might not understand your "call", prejudice, the legal system, and yourself (fears, inadequacies, selfishness, beliefs). This is just some of the opposition you may have to confront during your foster care journey.

Along with confrontation may come Criticism. As I have said several times, when you embrace the call of foster care on your life, you will encounter people who don't understand why you would subject yourself to the rigorous and emotional life of a foster parent. Sometimes, those "nay-sayers" are in your own family. I think Jeff's parents would agree that when we dropped the bomb on them (that we were going to be foster parents while we were parenting a six-year-old, a three-year-old and a two-year-old), their first thought was that we were crazy! Although they never said it, I knew they were wondering if I had heard "the call" correctly; if I had picked up the right telephone when the "call" came in. They were trying to protect us from ourselves. I have to qualify my comments by saying that my in-laws have always been very supportive of us. They often know our needs even before we do, and I have never seen a couple more willing to share what they have with anyone in need. They are so in tune with the needs of others and are filled with sheer joy when the Father allows them to meet one of those needs. They may kill me for saying this, but I've known them to give fifty-dollar and one-hundred-dollar tips at the local drive-in to hard-working women, just for the joy of it and the lasting gift that it gives them. They are the ultimate example of not "letting the left hand know what the right hand is doing." However, I think the beginning of our foster care journey was an endurance test for them: one of concern, fear, and at times frustration. I have to say that they passed that test with flying colors. Over the years they have embraced our cause as their own; they have supported us, prayed for us, loved on the babies that have been ours for a season, and, although at times it has been difficult, they have trusted the Spirit in us to do His will. I am eternally grateful for their love and support.

Cost. Serving God through serving the children in foster care will cost us something. The cost to each of us individually will vary, but it will cost nonetheless. It may be measured in time, in money, in grief, in giving up our own ambitions, in exhaustion; but whatever the cost, it can never compare to what we cost the Savior!

And finally: a Challenge. Do I feel that every Christian should be a foster or adoptive parent? No way. Do I feel that there are many people who have been called and have not yet answered the call? Absolutely. As believers, we are all aware of our commission to care for widows and orphans. Perhaps it is the word "orphan" that we don't associate with children in the United States in foster care. In my estimation, you do not have to be parentless to be an orphan. Foster children are orphans because they are, for a time at least, alone, powerless and without their parents. You don't have to look far to find children who are helpless, hopeless, alone and invisible.

And rest assured that the world is watching. Years ago we had an old van with a pro-life bumper-sticker; you know the one, "Abortion Stops a Beating Heart." I stuck it on the bumper and never really thought much more about it. That is, until one summer day at the neighborhood pool. I began talking with the mother of one of my son's classmates. This woman was from another country and was by all counts a liberal in her social and political thinking. Although we had casually known each other for a couple of years, she had never shared one of her first impressions of me. She said that she had seen me in the van with the bumper sticker and had thought to herself, "another pro-life kook" (my word, not hers) trying to tell women what to do and not do with their own bodies." But then, she said, she began to see me time and time again with different babies…different sexes, different races, different ages. When she got to know me, even casually, she got to know my heart, and more importantly, she got to "see" my heart. What a humbling experience as I tried to replay the times she could have seen me and wondered if my living testimony was always as it should have been. This incident showed me that what we say about pro-life issues is not nearly as important as what we do!

As believers, our responsibility does not end with saving a baby from the abortionist's hand. God continues to show me it is our obligation to care for children who are in desperate need of His help, His hope, and His healing; children of every age. Not only is it our responsibility to be pro-life before life, but it is also our responsibility to be pro-life throughout life. We as Christians cannot continue to let the burden of children in need fall on the government and then protest when the government doesn't get the job done. Let's think out of the box! Let's get out of our judgmental and legalistic state of mind and allow our heavenly Father to use us for His purposes.

When people find out that I am a foster parent, they inevitably say, "I could never do that! I'd want to keep every single one. Don't you get attached?" I know they are well-meaning, but after over fifteen years of those comments and questions, I must admit it drives me a little crazy. I want to say, "No, duh!" But, since I'm not normally a rude and sarcastic person, the Lord has given me another comeback: Yes, it is extremely difficult to let a child go that you have loved and cared for, but the Lord has shown me that that is exactly the person that needs to be taking care of these misplaced children. If I could separate myself from loving and attaching to the child and just feel like I am baby-sitting rather than being a real mother, God would never have called me to do this. So, maybe YOU are actually the perfect person to be a foster parent.

Usually they are a bit stunned at this point. However, a couple of years ago, I was speaking at an event for perspective foster and adoptive parents and shared my new found thesis on who should or should not be a foster parent. It was a large group of people, but only a few made a commitment to pursue this ministry. One couple approached me after the meeting was over and the wife began to share with me how she had come that evening with a lot of fear. She had told her husband the very things I stated earlier, that she didn't know if she could let a child go after loving and caring for him or her. She said that as I spoke she knew that what I said was said for her ears to hear. I was so excited to learn that what I thought was my new cunning retort actually broke through to meet a need in the life of someone that God had called to foster. What a praise!

According to the National Adoption Center, "There are no unwanted children, just unfound families." What about you? Are you one of those unfound families? What is your passion? As you read these words is there a stirring in your soul, a truth that resonates down deep within your being? Is God calling you to open your arms and your home for a season, or for a lifetime, to a child in need? If so, I want to challenge you to take the first step. Make a call to your local DHS office and find out what their needs are. Attend an informational meeting. Just take one little faith step at a time. And if you don't feel called to foster or adopt, there are so many ways you can support those who do feel called. You can pray, babysit, take a meal, or provide respite care. You can advocate for children by volunteering through the court system with CASA (Court Appointed Special Advocates), with literacy programs or after school programs, work with abstinence education or you can mentor a child in foster care. What is stopping you? Let me challenge you to step out of your comfort zone and make a difference! Let me challenge you to step up to the plate and speak up for a child. Let me challenge you to quit talking, quit thinking, quit complaining and just get busy. Most importantly, let me challenge you to seek the Lord and trust that He will accomplish what concerns you!

The Wrap Up

CHAPTER SEVENTEEN

*A*s I wind down my writing, I am reminded of that day fifteen years ago when my foster care journey began. To say that my life has changed dramatically since then would be a classic understatement. I have a beautiful nine-month-old foster daughter sleeping in another room, a precocious four-year-old running around entertaining everyone, three teenagers who are a constant source of joy, blessing and encouragement, and a very supportive grown-man son away at college. There have been a million tears cried, thousands of diapers changed, hundreds and hundreds of bottles made, and I have been blessed to be a temporary mother, a middle mom, to over forty foster children. But, one thing hasn't changed: God's call. Sure, He has refined it, transformed it, overhauled it and pushed it to new levels beyond my wildest imagination, but the premise is the same: "It's time for you, my child, to put some ACTION behind those empty pro-life words."

I was in the final stages of writing this book when a disturbing thing happened. The Lord took me to a place I had never been before, a place that was so dark, so very painful and yet such a reminder of why I have swathed myself in this ministry. For the sake of privacy, I really cannot go into the "what, where, when, why and how" of this situation; but for the sake of a little girl I'll call KeeKee, the story must be told. Through a supernatural circumstance, I found out about KeeKee: she'd been brought to a hospital in our area as a result of abuse. She wasn't even two years old yet. She was comatose. She was brain dead. She was alone. My heart reacted like a mother's. I asked the DHS worker if I could go and be with her (all the while wondering if I was really capable of going and being with her). The worker asked me with a surprised tone in her voice,

"Christie, is that what you want to do?"

"No," I admitted, "it's not what I want to do; it's what I have to do."

I told her I knew that Caryl, Donna, and Jan would be willing to help as well. A couple of hours after my conversation with the DHS worker, she and I met at the intensive care unit. I wasn't prepared for what I saw. There was Kee Kee; a beautiful, frail, angelic little girl. She was hooked up to every machine you could imagine with tubes coming out in every direction. I loved her from the minute I saw her. Although I would never see her with her eyes open, would never see her smile or hear her laugh, would never get the opportunity to have her skinny little arms wrap around my neck or her round little lips kiss my cheek. I loved her. I could not hold back; I immediately went to her side and began what would be a three-day ritual of rubbing her tiny face, holding her tiny hand in mine and telling her that everything was going to be all right. I felt my heart sink, I was nauseous; I wanted to scream at the top of my lungs, "How did this happen?" But, deep in my spirit, I knew that this was a divine appointment; it was no coincidence that I was at KeeKee's bedside. It was hard for me to wrap my mind around the fact that unless God intervened in a miraculous way, she was going to die, because lying there, she looked as if she were sleeping: so peaceful, so contented as the rhythmic motion of the ventilator and the air puffs of the warming blanket masked what was really going on. Caryl and I went back later in the day and stayed and stayed and stayed. We couldn't leave her. We tried to comfort each other, but nothing made sense. We just cried and prayed, cried and prayed. The next day, Jan joined us as we all spent the day at the hospital. The time came to do the neurological tests to determine whether or not there was any brain activity. Would we like to be with her while the test was done? Of course we would; we were her family now. The world stopped as the doctor unplugged the ventilator and hooked up the oxygen. Hovering around KeeKee's bed were two doctors, two nurses, a social worker, and the organ donation team director along with Caryl and me. For ten eternal minutes, sixteen eyes gazed at the tiny abdomen. I felt myself saying under my breath, "Breathe, breathe" between silent prayers for God to work a miracle. For ten minutes the abdomen lay flat; the tiny body, limp and lifeless. I didn't know if I could stand there, if I could hear what the doctor was going to say.

"There is no brain activity, I'm sorry," he said. With those words a sense of resolve came over me. I would never be the same. I prayed that my ministry would never be the same.

Caryl touched my shoulder and said, "Let's ask the doctor if we can hold her; I want to hold her; she needs someone to hold her."

The doctors were so gentle with us, so compassionate. They told us they had hoped that someone would hold her. In a few minutes the nurses made all of the arrangements; a rocking chair was brought in, the tubes and machines were adjusted, and KeeKee was placed in Caryl's arms. I will never forget that moment: the sight of Caryl cradling this beautiful innocent child, the sound of Caryl's weeping as she laid her body over KeeKee's, enfolding this little one in her arms, all the while rocking and promising her that we were there and we loved her. I remember thinking that KeeKee looked like an orphan from another country, one that you would see on television, but as my mind snapped back to reality, I realized that we were right here in our own city, living out this nightmare! And then, it was my turn. Lord knows, I have rocked a lot of babies. This time was not like any of the others. The depth of grief and despair was beyond my comprehension. The sense of loss was almost unbearable. The needlessness of the moment, the tragedy, and the heartbreak of what this tiny little girl had been through in her short life all flooded my thoughts. Then the resolve came to the surface again. I whispered to Kee Kee, "Your death will not be in vain, little one. I don't know what God wants to do with this, but your death will not be in vain." I sang to her and held her close. I wanted her to know we were there.

Jan, Caryl, and I made our way to our favorite children's clothing store. We all love to shop. We all love baby clothes. We love to tell each other about great deals and about beautiful new lines of clothing that will look great on our girls. But on this day, shopping was not a welcome activity, and shopping for a dress for KeeKee was anything but joyful. It was devastating, but KeeKee deserved the best. We prayed as we entered the store that we would find the perfect outfit for her, and we did: a beautiful white sundress with pink smocking and angel sleeves, ruffled socks and panties and a pink bow. Jan found a beautiful cross bracelet that completed KeeKee's "going home" outfit.

The day KeeKee died, I wrote these words about my feelings, "One part of me wants to shout this from the rooftops, for all of the world to hear — the truth about the injustice and how we as a society let her down, but the other part of me wants to keep this so close to my heart; an intimate part of my being, so close that I never, ever forget the face of a little girl who endured months of the worst that life had to offer, but ended up in the arms of the One that will never let her down."

The organ donation team was so empathetic. The director knew that we had only known KeeKee for two or three days, and yet somehow she seemed to understand our deep love for her. She asked if we would each like a copy of KeeKee's hand prints. We were expecting the ink pressed hands that the hospital makes for you when your baby is born. We were in for a surprise. What we got were clay-embossed handprints framed out in beautiful wood frames. The details of the hand prints made us cry: the tiny fingers, the distinct lines and wrinkles, and the imprint of the Band-Aid on her left thumb. My heart broke as I held the frame close, and yet there was something so comforting about having it, about getting to keep it forever.

Several days later, Jeff joined Jan, Caryl and me at the funeral home before KeeKee's service. Once again, I was struck by how perfect, how beautiful, how at peace KeeKee looked, and I almost thought I saw her breathe. The outfit was perfect, perfect for a little princess joining the heavenly choir of angels; a little princess that may not have been on this earth long, but made a lasting impact on a group of mothers that were honored to call her "daughter" for a short while. A week later, I wrote: "Today I asked the Lord to keep KeeKee's memory in front of me, not in a morbid way, but in an inspiring way that keeps me motivated, always fighting, always changing, always moving and always advocating for children like her."

Tomorrow I will make my way to KeeKee's grave, in honor of her second birthday. I pray that God will use her life to once again transform my life and deepen the roots of my ministry.

In closing, I have to ask some profound questions that, when answered with a look at the Father's blueprint, could rock our nation and change the course of history for thousands of children who are invisible to most of humanity. Nevertheless, these children deserve the best that life has to offer, the best that comes as a result of God's grace flowing through the hands of those of us to whom much has been given. How many children like KeeKee would have loving families if Christians really acted like Jesus? How many birth parents would see the love of God in Christian foster parents who love their children as their own? How would our government react if the foster care system was flooded with all of the foster parents it needed because the church stood up and was counted? What would happen if there were no children waiting to be adopted because God's people decided to bridge the gap? How many children would find forever families and ultimately be ushered into God's forever family? What an incredible testimony that would be.

I have to thank the Lord for allowing me the privilege of being a foster mom and adoptive mom. I have to thank my family and friends (you know who you are!) for joining me on this journey; for their love, support, encouragement and shoulders to cry on. I have to thank my precious children, Chase, Caleb, Cara, Connor and Serenity for not only supporting me, but for taking on this ministry as their own and passionately ensuring that we continue our pursuit to allow God to use us in the lives of children in our state. And I have to thank Jeff, my one-of-a-kind husband, who has been my rock, my advisor, my therapist, my fortress, my protector, my comedian, and my incredible partner in this ministry and in life!

I am looking forward to the continuation of this journey. My life has been richly blessed because I have seen the miraculous. The naivety that I once owned has long gone away. This world is sinful, this world wants to destroy, this world wants failure and complacency, but we as Christians have overcome all of those things! We have the distinct honor of bringing freedom, restoration, success and genuine love and dignity to children who richly deserve to experience life the way the Maker intended. I heard a quote recently at a meeting regarding foster care, a quote of unknown origin: "If not you, who? If not now, when?" There may be no one else. There may be no other time. Is this your time to embrace God's purpose and plan for your life as it relates to the orphans in your community? Won't you join me and make a difference in the life of a child? They are counting on us. The "who" is you. And the time is now.

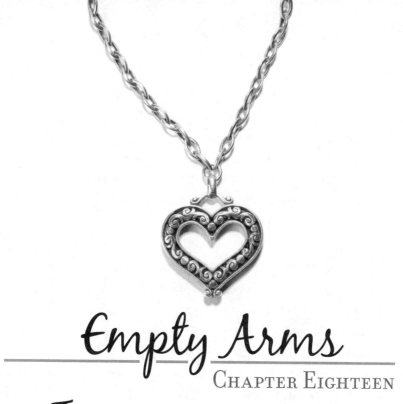

Empty Arms

CHAPTER EIGHTEEN

$\mathcal{T}$he manuscript was complete, the editing was done, the printing and publishing quote was in, the graphic artist was chosen for the cover, and it seemed that everything was on go. However, exactly one month, three days and eight hours ago, things changed. Another story happened, another piece to the puzzle, another strand in the tapestry of my ministry, another chapter in my story, and it has to be told. Even now, as I sit with my hands on the keyboard, I'm not sure I have the strength to tell this story. I feel the knot in my throat; tears well up in my eyes and my heart beats faster as I anticipate actually seeing this chapter in print. Nevertheless, if I am going to do what I set out to do in the beginning of this book, that is to truly be transparent, to lay all my cards on the table, then I must conjure up every-thing that is within me — all of the truths the heavenly Father has taught me — in order to let my heart spill out onto this page.

This is the story of a little girl I'll call Baby B.

I will never, ever forget the day I got the call about B. Jeff and I were sitting in a parenting conference at our church. Serenity's adoption was still not final, and we were fostering her one year old brother at the time. As I sat in the conference with my cell phone on silent, I looked down and saw that I had received a call from Serenity's caseworker. "Interesting," I thought, "on a Saturday." I excused myself and went to the foyer to return her call.

"Everything is fine with Serenity's case," she said, "I just wondered if you knew of anyone, Christie, who would be willing to take a five-week-old baby girl?"

"Well, not me!" I thought. "Who do you think I am, the old woman that lives in the shoe?"

"I can't think of anyone right now," were the words that *actually* came out of my mouth, "but, I will make a couple of phone calls to see if anyone I know can take her, and I'll call you right back."

I made the phone calls, but had no success in finding a family for this baby. So, I did what I considered the next best thing, I asked Jeff if we could take her for the weekend. He looked at me as he often does when I come to him with one of my emotional schemes, but as usual he agreed that we would take her for the weekend. I would call the caseworker on Monday and she would find a permanent placement for this baby.

I immediately went into "baby mode." I left the conference early, rushed home to get my infant car seat and headed to DHS. There, in the arms of the caseworker was the most beautiful newborn baby girl with curly hair and chubby cheeks and all dressed in lime green.

"Uh-Oh."

I'm sure I don't need to tell you what happened next. On Sunday night Jeff looked at me and said seven words that would change my life:

"You want to try this, don't you?"

As crazy as it sounded, taking on another baby with the chaos of a preschooler with ADHD, an incredibly active one year old and four other children going in four different directions, I found myself saying yes. I really believe it was my heart answering, not my mouth. I knew deep down in my soul that this was our daughter and she belonged in my arms; I just didn't know for how long.

The event that brought Baby B into foster care was horrific. Though by God's grace she was not harmed, it was a violent act that could have been catastrophic. That truth made me hold her tighter and love her deeper. It also filled me with a deep resolve that no one would ever, ever be in a position to hurt her again.

Little did I know how tight my hold on this precious one would become, how deep my love would root and how intense my resolve would tunnel down into the very core of my being. Baby B was the perfect baby. She slept like a log. She was content. She spit up a lot, but hey, nobody's perfect! She was a little "snuggle bunny" who was so easy going. We began to notice that she seemed a bit too easy going. She would sleep long hours at a time and never seemed to wake during the night, even with the high pitched screams of our one year old son. Jeff and I became very concerned about her hearing. We had her hearing tested; she failed. We had her hearing tested again; she failed again. We went to a specialist and had her hearing tested; she failed.

Bless her heart, she will probably be in therapy later in life for all the ways we tested her hearing ourselves: loud screams, sudden whistles, books dropped on the floor, her name broadcast at mega decibels from every part of the room. And yet, she wasn't hearing us. Although I know many people thrive in and through their deafness, I couldn't help but grieve as I thought about her life without sound. For some reason, it was her not hearing music and our voices that grieved me the most. Jeff began to pray that God would take care of whatever was causing the problem or just miraculously heal her as only He could do. When she was five months old, we returned to the specialist to have her tested again; she passed. God had done it; our girl could hear!

Next, B's difficulty with swallowing almost required a feeding tube. And because of the months of not hearing, she was speech and language delayed. But other than that, she was growing and was way ahead of the curve in height and weight. She had her own fashion sense (okay, I had my own fashion sense for her). She looked beautiful in lime, orange, and fuchsia—and even better in a combination of the three. And as with any girl that resides in the Erwin household, she never left home without a bow. Everywhere I went people talked about how gorgeous she was. Our family bonded with her quickly and deeply.

B's case was complicated by the incident that brought her into care, by mental illness and by a history of family members that didn't get along. We began a roller coaster ride that was all too familiar to us. A few weeks after she came into our home, it seemed as if she would be leaving us to go and live with a relative, but then the tracks turned downward, and that plan was scrapped. Paternity was established, and she began visits with her biological mother and father as well as with a couple of extended family members. The tension within the family was palpable, and the internal hostility infiltrated the whole case. As time marched on, it seemed as if there was no straightforward plan for the future of this baby.

Meanwhile, we loved every minute as B was growing and changing. We hung on every little sound that eked out of her mouth. I learned that styling her hair, which was so very different in texture from Serenity's, was a breeze. We watched her learn to crawl, to pull up, and play patty-cake. We were there when she got her first tooth and then a mouthful of teeth. (She drooled constantly. Jeff said that wherever she crawled, she left a trail, like a slug.) We cheered as she took her first step, and we hosted her first birthday party where everything from her dress and bloomers to the two cakes were pink and green polka dots. We watched as her love for books bloomed, and our hearts overflowed as we observed the way she tenderly rocked her baby dolls. She loved her blankets, so we bought every ultra soft blanket we could find. She would pull them all into her crib at night and be lying on top of the blanket mountain in the morning. When she was tired, her blanket would go up to her face and her thumb would go into her mouth. She even adopted one of Serenity's silk dresses as a pseudo-blankie. She'd grab any purse, bag, infant carrier, whatever, and throw it over her arm like it was a genuine Coach or Dooney and Bourke, and she was a princess!

We had the distinct pleasure of being her favorite audience as she learned to dance with the grace and humor that only a one-year-old can. We laughed our heads off as she and Serenity performed their musical theatre, complete with a boom box and High School Musical CD, for all of us as we sat in the living room. I was the recipient of her first kiss as she leaned into my cheek and smacked "MMMM-MA." B and I were inseparable as we shopped, ran errands, picked up kids and moved the Heart Gallery together. Cara called her "pipsqueak." When Chase and

Caleb came home from college on the weekends, she would run into their arms with a huge smile. Connor loved her with an undying love. Serenity loved to mother her, almost as much as I did. The small group of newlyweds that Jeff and I lead on Sunday nights nurtured her, loved her and fed her every week. She would move from one set of arms to the next and always knew that the guys in the group were the softies who would feed her the most! They felt like they were her extended parents. B was well loved, and we were all well loved by her.

The decision was made by DHS and the courts to terminate parental rights. All of the parties in the case were on board in a passionate unified way that I had never seen at DHS. (Except the birth parents attorneys of course, who wanted her placed with a relative.) We made our way to court for the termination hearing, fifteen months after B came to live with us. Arguments were made, questions were asked, positions were taken, and the outcome, the very destiny of this child's life, was left in the hands of one woman: the judge.

Although I haven't said it up to this point, I'm sure you have read between the lines and know our position: This is our daughter and we want her to be our daughter forever.

It is very important to note that when reunification had been the goal, we were on that team. But, once the goal in B's case was changed to adoption, our hearts and minds turned towards adoption as well. I had picked out her name months before (okay, maybe my heart had "turned" a little ahead of schedule). Cara and I had kept the name to ourselves for awhile before letting Daddy in on it — Emme Camryn. Granted the "C" name wouldn't be first this time, but it would be there nonetheless. I looked on the Internet one night to see what Emme meant and it was defined as "whole, complete." "It's a sign," I thought.

CHAPTER 18: *Empty Arms*

Once B is added to the Erwin gang, our family will be whole and complete: Three girls and three boys — a modern day "Brady Bunch." I rehearsed the names of our new family over and over in my mind: Chase Sullivan, Caleb Saeger, Cara Elizabeth, Connor Scott, Caroline Serenity and Emme Camryn. Wow! That had a ring to it.

No new court date was set; all we had to do was *wait* for the judge's ruling. All we had to do was wait for the judge's ruling. For five weeks we waited with bated breath.

It seemed like any time I ran into anyone involved in the case from DHS they would say, "I don't think you have anything to worry about, I can't imagine the judge deciding to do anything but terminate."

On a Wednesday afternoon, I was loading B and Serenity in the car to head to the dentist's office. My cell phone rang, and my life would never be the same. B's attorney was on the other end of the line.

"Christie, the judge has decided to send B to the relative," she managed to mutter. "I'm sorry."

To say I was in shock would be an understatement of epic proportion. I fumbled with my purse and the diaper bag, clumsily got B out of her car seat, grabbed Serenity's hand and nervously led them back into the house. "I've got to call Jeff," I thought as I dialed his number.

"They are sending B to the relative," I heard myself say, all the while wondering if I was really saying those words.

"I'll be right there," he said. And he was. Chase was home from college working at Jeff's office. He, too, was at my side in a matter of minutes.

I paced. I cried. I held my baby daughter tight. I saw confusion in Serenity's eyes.

"How am I going to do this?" I shouted. "How are we going to do this? I can't call the kids at school and have them come home. Cara can't drive with this on her mind," I reasoned.

When I finally got the caseworker on the phone, she informed me that the relative wanted B immediately. The caseworker was devastated, as well, and wondered what I wanted to do. I told her that there was no way I could drive my daughter to a strange place with all of her worldly belongings and leave her. She would have to pick her up.

So, for the next three hours, I gathered her things. I washed her clothes and cried, I picked up her dolls, stuffed animals, and her little bike and cried: I held her blankets and "silkies" tight and cried: I organized her precious books, packed all of her clothes and cried. I sent Jeff to the store for extra diapers and an extra duffle bag and cried. I wrapped myself around this precious gift that God had entrusted to me and wept. I could not imagine my life without her.

The hour that followed is forever etched in my mind. Our family gathered for a prayer time. Jeff cried out to the Father amid silent sobs and sniffles. B didn't have a clue what was happening, and I am sure wondered if her entire family had gone totally insane! She wandered from person to person as Daddy prayed. My parents came over and held us. My six-year-old nephew came to say goodbye. The caseworker arrived and the boys loaded the car. It was time.

And time stood still. I will never forget the utter hopelessness and helplessness I felt as Jeff and I made our way to the waiting car with our daughter. Our entire family was on the porch. I felt as if I was moving in slow motion. I put her in the car seat, buckled her in tight, and kissed her. My weeping was uncontrollable. My heart was shattered. B looked at us with a question mark as we told her how much we loved her and shut the door. The car drove away with my hopes and dreams inside.

There are no words to describe what these last weeks have been. We have lost something priceless. We have lost a daughter. At this point in time, there is nothing anyone can say or do to change that. We have experienced a death of another sort; on one hand there is a sense of finality and on the other, no closure.

It seems that with every store I enter, there is a reminder of the emptiness, of what I am missing: the baby food aisle, the toy section, everything at Baby Gap and even looking at the shopping carts makes me hyperventilate. Cara says I have made friends at all of my favorite stores, and I really can't disagree with her. I tend to stand out with my babies, which leads to great conversations and opportunities to share my heart. I was in Target not long after B left when one of my store friends asked me where my baby was. I told her what had happened and with open arms she embraced me, told me she was so sorry, even called me "Boo" and said, "You just don't look right without your baby."

We have never had this kind of grief. "Yes, you have," you may say. "It's in the book!" The grief caused by the loss of a child, yes. But, not the grief caused by the loss of a child that we thought would be ours forever. We had known in all of the cases up to this point that the child would either be adopted by a forever family or be returned home to his/her biological family; but this time it was different.

I have seen snapshots of B in my mind at every turn: her face as she took our hands in hers while playing patty-cake and her tiny pursed mouth as she tried to say "roll it up", her little round bottom grooving to the music, her thumb in her mouth as she put her head on my shoulder, her eyes peering over the baby bed watching Jeff's morning routine and him kissing her as he left for work, her horrified look when she feared our Golden Retrievers would run into the house and eat her alive, her crinkled lips and turned up nose when she tried a new food, her chubby little hands reaching out for me, the excitement in her eyes when we picked her up from her Sunday school class, and the list goes on and on. At night as I move in the darkness towards my bed, I run my hand along her bed rail and imagine her little hands holding on, waiting for me to pick her up. I have literally had to catch my breath with grief. There have been times when I have paced around the house uncertain of what to do. I have written down Scriptures about hope and strewn them throughout the house. The loss is palpable. The future uncertain. Her destiny unsure.

Unsure by my measuring stick, but there is One to whom nothing is unsure. One to whom no future is uncertain. One to whom there is no coincidence, no happenstance, no "luck of the draw," no karma or kismet, to whom nothing is a fluke. In the midst of it all, He has been here. He has wrapped His arms around me and held me tight. When I shouted aloud to Him, "I don't trust this situation!" He whispered back, "But you can trust Me." He has seen the ugliness of my despair and felt the literal aching of my arms just to hold my child. He has known my doubts and fears, tolerated my questions, witnessed my self-ishness and disillusionment, felt my heartbreak, caught my tears and yet purposed in His heart to work out His plan in me, even when my purpose, my passion, my calling, and the course of my life seemed unclear. And for that I am eternally grateful.

Though this case is not over and, really, anything could happen, in spite of it all, I am eternally grateful for something else. I am grateful for a "weekend baby" who captured my heart and the hearts of my family; a baby that regardless of proximity, is our daughter forever, period. Nothing and no one can take that away from us. I pray that in her tiny heart she will always sense our love, feel our prayers, and be able to grasp how deep our commitment to her was and is. And one last thing I pray: that this is not really the end of this chapter, that there will be more of this story to tell, more supernatural events to recount, and in the end all of the glory will shine on the heavenly Father who is "able to do far more than we would ever dare to ask or even dream of — infinitely beyond our highest prayers, desires, thoughts, or hopes." (Ephesians 3:20 The Way, The Living Bible)

Appendix

For more information about foster care and adoption, please contact your state's Department of Human Services; Division of Children and Family, a foster care/adoption agency in your area, or one of the following:

Adopt US Kids

www.adoptuskids.org   1-800-200-4005

The mission of AdoptUsKids is to recruit and connect foster and adoptive families with waiting children throughout the United States.

Bethany Christian Services

www.Bethany.org   1-800-BETHANY

Bethany Christian Services is a Christ-centered, not-for-profit, pro-life, adoption and family services agency with more than 75 locations in 32 states and ministries in more than a dozen countries.

Focus on the Family
Orphan Care Initiative

www.iCareAboutOrphans.org   1-800-A-FAMILY (232-6459)

At Focus on the Family, we believe that every child deserves to know the love of a forever family. Therefore, the primary objective of the Adoption & Orphan Care Initiative is to raise awareness of and recruit families for these waiting children. In addition, we work to provide best-in-class post-placement resources and support to adoptive families.

HEART GALLERY OF AMERICA

www.heartgalleryofamerica.org

The Heart Gallery is a traveling photographic and audio exhibit created to find forever families for children in foster care. The Heart Gallery of America is a collaborative project of over 120 Heart Galleries across the United States (and growing) designed to increase the number of adoptive families for children needing homes in our community.

HOPE FOR ORPHANS,
A MINISTRY OF FAMILYLIFE

www.hopefororphans.org   1-800-FL-TODAY

Hope for Orphans exists to help you and your church do what God has called you to do for children in foster care and for orphans around the world. We have a variety of materials designed to help prepare followers of Christ for adoption, foster care and church-based orphans ministry.

WWW.THEMIDDLEMOM.COM